Probation Violations in North Carolina

James M. Markham   2018

The School of Government at the University of North Carolina at Chapel Hill works to improve the lives of North Carolinians by engaging in practical scholarship that helps public officials and citizens understand and improve state and local government. Established in 1931 as the Institute of Government, the School provides educational, advisory, and research services for state and local governments. The School of Government is also home to a nationally ranked Master of Public Administration program, the North Carolina Judicial College, and specialized centers focused on community and economic development, information technology, and environmental finance.

As the largest university-based local government training, advisory, and research organization in the United States, the School of Government offers up to 200 courses, webinars, and specialized conferences for more than 12,000 public officials each year. In addition, faculty members annually publish approximately 50 books, manuals, reports, articles, bulletins, and other print and online content related to state and local government. The School also produces the *Daily Bulletin Online* each day the General Assembly is in session, reporting on activities for members of the legislature and others who need to follow the course of legislation.

Operating support for the School of Government's programs and activities comes from many sources, including state appropriations, local government membership dues, private contributions, publication sales, course fees, and service contracts.

Visit sog.unc.edu or call 919.966.5381 for more information on the School's courses, publications, programs, and services.

Michael R. Smith, DEAN
Thomas H. Thornburg, SENIOR ASSOCIATE DEAN
Jen Willis, ASSOCIATE DEAN FOR DEVELOPMENT
Michael Vollmer, ASSOCIATE DEAN FOR ADMINISTRATION

FACULTY

Whitney Afonso
Trey Allen
Gregory S. Allison
David N. Ammons
Ann M. Anderson
Maureen Berner
Frayda S. Bluestein
Mark F. Botts
Anita R. Brown-Graham
Peg Carlson
Leisha DeHart-Davis
Shea Riggsbee Denning
Sara DePasquale
James C. Drennan
Richard D. Ducker

Jacquelyn Greene
Norma Houston
Cheryl Daniels Howell
Jeffrey A. Hughes
Willow S. Jacobson
Robert P. Joyce
Diane M. Juffras
Dona G. Lewandowski
Adam Lovelady
James M. Markham
Christopher B. McLaughlin
Kara A. Millonzi
Jill D. Moore
Jonathan Q. Morgan
Ricardo S. Morse

C. Tyler Mulligan
Kimberly L. Nelson
David W. Owens
William C. Rivenbark
Dale J. Roenigk
John Rubin
Jessica Smith
Meredith Smith
Carl W. Stenberg III
John B. Stephens
Charles Szypszak
Shannon H. Tufts
Aimee N. Wall
Jeffrey B. Welty
Richard B. Whisnant

Printed in the United States of America

22 21 20 19 18   1 2 3 4 5

ISBN 978-1-56011-941-8

Contents

I. Introduction

A defendant sentenced to probation is subject to conditions that he or she must follow as part of the sentence. A willful failure to comply with those conditions is a violation of probation. The court can respond to a violation in many ways, ranging from doing nothing to—in certain circumstances—revoking probation and activating the defendant's suspended sentence. Before the court can take action, however, a probationer is entitled to notice and a hearing at which the court will determine whether a violation occurred.

This book sets out the law applicable to probation violation hearings in North Carolina. A probation violation hearing is less formal than a criminal trial, but it still requires certain procedures as a matter of state statute and constitutional due process. The traditional view, expressed in many older cases, was that probation was an "act of grace" by the state and that a defendant therefore had little basis upon which to attack any perceived unfairness in the revocation process.[1] Probation was considered a privilege, not a right.

That view was expressly rejected by the Supreme Court of the United States in the early 1970s in *Morrissey v. Brewer*[2] and *Gagnon v. Scarpelli*,[3] which set out a new framework for the process due before a person's probation could be revoked. The rights and procedures described in those cases—written notice of alleged violations, a preliminary hearing, an opportunity to be heard by a neutral and detached officer, and in some cases counsel—were codified into North Carolina law in 1977.[4]

From the late 1970s until 2011, the laws and procedures applicable to probation violations did not change much. Provided the proper procedures were followed, a judge had broad discretion to respond to any single violation by revoking the defendant's probation and activating his or her suspended sentence. In 2011, the General Assembly passed the Justice Reinvestment Act, making major changes to the law of sentencing and probation.[5] The revised law placed substantial limitations on a judge's authority to revoke probation for violations other than a new criminal offense or absconding, as discussed below.

Unless otherwise indicated, the law and procedures described in this book apply to supervised and unsupervised probation alike and to cases sentenced under both Structured Sentencing and the impaired driving law.[6] The procedures do not, however, apply to alleged violations of post-release supervision or parole. Those violations

---

1. *See, e.g.,* State v. Duncan, 270 N.C. 241 (1967).
2. 408 U.S. 471 (1972).
3. 411 U.S. 778 (1973).
4. *See* N.C. GEN. STAT. (hereinafter G.S.) § 15A-1345 (explicitly described in the Official Commentary as responding primarily to the dictates of *Gagnon* and *Morrissey*).
5. *See generally* JAMES M. MARKHAM, THE NORTH CAROLINA JUSTICE REINVESTMENT ACT (UNC School of Government, 2012).
6. G.S. 15A-1341(a).

are handled under similar but statutorily separate procedures outlined in Article 84A (post-release supervision) and Article 85 (parole) of G.S. Chapter 15A.[7]

II. Initiating a Violation

A. Alleging a Violation

In supervised probation cases, the violation process typically begins when a probation officer files a violation report (Form DCC-10) with the clerk of court. The State must give the probationer notice of the violation hearing and its purpose, including a statement of the violations alleged, at least 24 hours before the hearing, unless such notice is waived by the probationer.[8] The DCC-10 constitutes notice of the alleged violations and controls the scope of the ensuing hearing. The court is empowered to act only on violating behavior alleged in the notice provided to the defendant.[9]

A violation report must include a "statement of the violations alleged."[10] It need not be written with the technical precision of an indictment, but it must give the defendant sufficient information about the allegedly offending behavior to allow him or her to prepare a defense. A failure to identify the precise condition violated does not invalidate a violation report,[11] but the better practice for the officer is surely to expressly state which condition of probation has been violated, and to connect the violating behavior to that condition. Even if not required as a matter of proper notice under G.S. 15A-1345(e), identification of the specific condition violated is required as part of the written statement an officer prepares in conjunction with a probationer's arrest under G.S. 15A-1345(a).

Sometimes a probation officer will allege a violation of the "commit no criminal offense" condition by reference to the fact that the probationer has criminal charges pending for the behavior. Under Department of Public Safety administrative policy, the preferred practice is for the officer to frame the violation around the criminal behavior itself—for example, to allege that "the defendant drove while impaired,"

---

7. *See* Jamie Markham, *The Post-Release Supervision Violation Hearing Process in a Nutshell*, UNC Sch. of Gov't: N.C. Crim. L. Blog (Feb. 27, 2013), http:// nccriminallaw.sog.unc.edu/the-post-release-supervision-violation-hearing-process-in-a-nutshell.

8. G.S. 15A-1345(e).

9. State v. Cunningham, 63 N.C. App. 470 (1983) (reversing a defendant's revocation based on trespass and damage to real property when the violation report alleged only that he had played loud music and removed signs posted by his neighbors).

10. G.S. 15A-1345(e).

11. State v. Moore, 370 N.C. 338 (2017). In *Moore*, the probation officer alleged a new criminal offense violation under the heading "Other Violation," without specifically stating that the defendant violated the "commit no criminal offense" condition. The supreme court concluded that the violation report was valid, in that G.S. 15A-1345(e) requires only allegation of the behavior that violates a condition, not identification of the condition itself.

rather than alleging that the defendant has "pending charges for DWI." Alleging the violation in that way helps avoid any later sense that the probationer is being revoked solely based on the pendency of a criminal charge.[12] However, as far as proper notice goes, a probation officer's reference to a pending charge does not spoil an otherwise proper violation report.[13]

Though no statute expressly says so, a prosecutor probably may allege a violation of probation. If so, the ordinary rules for notice and timing would apply.[14]

B. Alleging a Violation of Unsupervised Probation

In cases of unsupervised probation, violations are generally reported to the court by the clerk's office or by community service staff. Notice of a hearing in response to a violation of unsupervised probation must be given by either personal delivery to the probationer or by U.S. mail to the last known address available to the preparer of the notice and reasonably believed to provide actual notice. If mailed, the notice must be sent at least 10 days prior to any hearing and must state the nature of the violation.[15] Form AOC-CR-220 may be used to provide notice of a hearing on a violation of unsupervised probation. If notice is given by mail and the defendant does not appear, the court may either terminate probation and enter appropriate orders for the enforcement of any outstanding monetary obligations (as otherwise provided by law), or provide for other notice to the defendant as provided in G.S. Chapter 15A.[16]

Community service staff must report significant violations of cases under their purview either in person or by mail as provided in G.S. 143B-708(e). In those cases, the court must conduct a hearing even if the person ordered to perform community service fails to appear. If the court determines that there was a willful failure to comply, it must revoke the person's driver's license until the community service requirement is met. Only when the person is present, however, may the court take other actions generally authorized in response to violations of probation.[17]

---

12. *See infra* notes 112–123 and accompanying text for a full discussion of the issue of new criminal offense violations based on pending charges that have not yet resulted in a conviction.

13. State v. Lee, 232 N.C. App. 256 (2014) ("The violation report identified the criminal offense on which the trial court relied to revoke defendant's probation—possession of a firearm by a felon—and the specific county and case file number of that alleged offense. Given such notice, defendant was aware that the State was alleging a revocation-eligible violation and he was aware of the exact violation upon which the State relied."), *overruled on other grounds,* State v. Moore, 370 N.C. 338 (2017).

14. *See* G.S. 15A-1344(e) (providing that "the State" must give the probationer notice of the hearing and its purpose).

15. G.S. 15A-1344(b1)(1).

16. G.S. 15A-1344(b1)(2).

17. G.S. 143B-708(e).

C. Notice of Failures to Pay Child Support as a Condition of Probation

A special statutory provision, G.S. 15A-1344.1, sets out a procedure to ensure payments of child support ordered as a condition of probation. When a court requires a defendant to support his or her children—a regular condition of probation under G.S. 15A-1343(b)(4)—the court is also empowered under G.S. 15A-1344.1(a) to order that support payments be made to the State Child Support Collection and Disbursement Unit for remittance to the party entitled to receive the payments. If a court enters such an order, the clerk of court must maintain records related to the payments.[18] The law then sets out procedures, different for IV-D (referencing Title IV-D of the federal Social Security Act, which provides for state child support systems) and non-IV-D cases, through which the clerk of superior court may notify the defendant of any arrearage in the required payments. If the arrearage is not paid in full, the law requires the clerk to notify the district attorney and the defendant's probation officer, who must then initiate revocation proceedings, make a motion for income withholding under G.S. 110-136.5, or both.[19]

For a variety of reasons, the special procedures set out in G.S. 15A-1344.1 are no longer used as a practical matter. Due to the evolution of centralized child support enforcement over the years, judges no longer need to order in the criminal case that payments be made to the State Child Support Collection and Disbursement Unit; centralized collection is now the default. The special notice procedures set out in G.S. 15A-1344.1(d) are also generally unnecessary, as immediate income withholding is effectively automatic under G.S. 110-136.5. Thus, probation officers and court officials are much more likely to give notice of alleged violations related to child support obligations through the same mechanisms applicable to other violations—a violation report by the probation officer or a notice of violation of unsupervised probation, depending on whether the case is one of supervised or unsupervised probation.

D. Dismissing a Violation

No specific statute governs the dismissal of probation violations. Nevertheless, courts routinely dismiss violations after a hearing where the violations are not found, or when a court chooses not to act on a violation. It is also generally understood that a prosecutor may dismiss a probation violation—or at least effectively dismiss it by choosing not to prosecute it. Agreed-upon resolutions of probation matters are often included in plea arrangements between the State and a defendant regarding new criminal charges. As a practical matter, court computer systems will allow a probation violation to be dismissed with leave under G.S. 15A-932, but not voluntarily dismissed under G.S. 15A-931. As a result, local practice in the handling of dismissals of violations varies.

---

18. G.S. 15A-1344.1(b).
19. G.S. 15A-1344.1(d).

A defendant is not entitled to a continuance under G.S. 15A-1023 on matters related to probation when a trial judge rejects a plea bargain in a new criminal case that includes an agreement to continue the defendant on probation in a prior case.[20]

E. Addenda

There is no special statutory rule for amending a violation report. A probationer is entitled to notice of later-alleged violations in the same manner as any violations alleged in the first instance, including all requirements of timeliness, as discussed below.[21] The filing of an initial violation before a case expires does not preserve the authority to modify that violation or file additional violations once the case has expired.

F. Arrest or Citation

A supervised probationer is subject to arrest for violation of a condition of probation by a law enforcement officer or by a probation officer.[22] One of two documents typically authorizes the arrest. The first is an order for arrest issued by a judicial official.[23] The second is the written request of a probation officer (referred to by probation officers as an "authority to arrest," set out on Form DCC-12).[24] Either document must be accompanied by a written violation report, signed by the probation officer, alleging that the defendant has violated specific conditions of his or her probation. A probation officer may also arrest a probationer without a written order or motion when the officer has probable cause to believe that a violation has occurred,[25] although the policy of the Community Corrections Section of the Division of Adult Correction and Juvenile Justice (DACJJ) expresses a strong preference that officers seek an order for arrest or complete a DCC-12 before arresting a probationer.[26]

In general, a probation officer has the same powers of arrest as a sheriff in the execution of his or her duties,[27] probably including cases supervised pursuant to a deferred prosecution agreement or conditional discharge.[28] Probation officers should

---

20. State v. Cleary, 213 N.C. App. 198 (2011).

21. *See infra* notes 35–49 and accompanying text.

22. G.S. 15A-1345(a).

23. G.S. 15A-305(b)(4).

24. G.S. 15A-1345(a). By policy, an authority to arrest document is valid for only three days. If the document is not served on the probationer within three days, officers are instructed to seek an order for arrest from a judicial official. N.C. Dep't of Pub. Safety, Div. of Adult Corr. and Juvenile Justice, Section of Comty. Corr., Policy & Procedure Manual (2018) § D.0404 (hereinafter Community Corrections Policy).

25. State v. Waller, 37 N.C. App. 133 (1978).

26. Community Corrections Policy, *supra* note 24, § D.0404.

27. G.S. 15-205.

28. *See* Jamie Markham, *Probation Officers' Arrest Authority in Deferral Cases*, UNC Sch. of Gov't: N.C. Crim. L. Blog (Feb. 14, 2013), http://nccriminallaw.sog.unc.edu/probation-officers-arrest-authority-in-deferral-cases.

be considered state officers within the meaning of G.S. 15A-402(a), meaning that when they have the power to arrest, they may do so anywhere within the state of North Carolina. By policy, an officer may arrest a probationer only when the officer has reasonable suspicion that the probationer violated a condition of probation.[29]

It is not strictly necessary for an officer to arrest a probationer in advance of a violation hearing.[30] If the probation officer does not think it necessary to arrest the probationer, the probationer is given notice of the alleged violations and the time and place of the hearing and cited to court.

A probationer is not subject to arrest for a violation of probation if it is based on an offense for which he or she would be immune from prosecution under the drug-overdose "Good Samaritan" law. That law applies only to certain offenses (misdemeanor drug possession, felony possession of less than one gram of cocaine or heroin, and possession of drug paraphernalia), and only when evidence of the offense was obtained as the result of a person seeking medical assistance for a drug-related overdose.[31]

G. Bail for Alleged Probation Violators

A probationer arrested for an alleged violation of probation must be taken without unnecessary delay before a judicial official to have conditions of release set in the same manner as provided in G.S. 15A-534 for criminal charges.[32]

Some probationers are subject to rules that potentially delay the setting of release conditions. If a probationer either has pending charges for a felony offense or has ever been convicted of an offense that would be a reportable sex crime if committed today, the judicial official setting release conditions must, before imposing conditions of release, determine and record in writing whether the probationer poses a danger to the public. If the judicial official finds the probationer poses a danger to the public, the probationer must be denied release pending a revocation hearing. If the probationer does not pose a danger, release conditions are set as usual. If the judicial official has insufficient information to determine whether the probationer poses a danger, the probationer may be held for up to 7 days from the date of arrest so that the judicial official, or a subsequent reviewing judicial official, may obtain sufficient information to determine whether the probationer poses a threat to the public.[33] The requisite findings can be recorded on side two of Form AOC-CR-272.

---

29. COMMUNITY CORRECTIONS POLICY, *supra* note 24, § D.0403(a). The policy-based reasonable suspicion standard matches the standard required as a matter of federal constitutional law. *See* Jones v. Chandrasuwan, 820 F.3d 685 (4th Cir. 2016) (holding that probation officers must have reasonable suspicion before seeking a probationer's arrest, and that the officers in this case did not have reasonable suspicion to arrest the probationer for failing to pay his costs and fees).

30. G.S. 15A-1345(a).

31. G.S. 90-96.2.

32. G.S. 15A-1345(b).

33. G.S. 15A-1345(b1).

Sometimes the sentencing judge will order in the judgment suspending sentence or an order for arrest that a particular bond be set for a defendant in the event of his or her arrest for an alleged violation of probation, or that the defendant should be held without bond. The court has no clear authority to set an anticipatory bond in that way, and the court of appeals has urged caution on the part of the trial courts regarding this practice.[34] To the extent that the sentencing court or the judicial official issuing an order for arrest wishes to address the issue of prehearing release for a violation, the better practice is to recommend—not order—a bond in a certain amount.

H. Failures to Appear; Suspension of Public Assistance

When a probationer fails to appear for a probation violation hearing, the court may issue an order for arrest under G.S. 15A-305(4). A hearing extending or modifying probation may be held in the absence of a probationer who fails to appear after a reasonable effort has been made to notify him or her.[35] Probation should not, however, be revoked in the defendant's absence.

If an unsupervised probationer does not appear in response to a mailed notice, the court may either (a) terminate the probation and enter appropriate orders for the enforcement of any outstanding monetary obligations as otherwise provided by law or (b) provide for other notice to the person as authorized by G.S. Chapter 15A for a violation of probation.[36]

The court may order the suspension of any public assistance benefits being received by a probationer for whom the court has issued an order for arrest for violating probation but who is absconding or otherwise willfully avoiding arrest.[37] The suspension continues until the probationer surrenders or is otherwise brought under the court's jurisdiction. The court may use Form AOC-CR-650, *Order of Suspension of Public Benefits for Absconder*, to order the suspension. The suspension does not affect the eligibility for public assistance benefits being received by or for the benefit of a family member of the probationer.

I. Notice to Victims

For crimes covered under the Crime Victims' Rights Act (listed in G.S. 15A-830(a)(7)), a victim may elect to receive notice of certain post-trial proceedings involving the defendant, including probation violation hearings.[38] If a victim has elected to receive

---

34. *See* State v. Hilbert, 145 N.C. App. 440 (2001) (noting that the sentencing judge's order that the defendant be arrested and placed under a $100,000 cash bond in response to his first positive drug screen was against the better practice; at most, the sentencing judge could recommend, not order, a particular bond).

35. G.S. 15A-1344(d).

36. G.S. 15A-1344(b1).

37. G.S. 15A-1345(a1).

38. G.S. 15A-832.

notifications, Community Corrections must provide him or her with notice of, among other things, the date and location of any hearing to determine whether the defendant's supervision should be revoked, continued, modified, or terminated; the final disposition of any hearing; any modification of restitution; and the addition of any intermediate sanction. The notification must be provided within 30 days of the event requiring notification.[39]

III. Violation Hearings

A. Jurisdiction

A court's jurisdiction to review a probationer's compliance with the terms of his or her probation is limited by statute. The court has power to act "any time prior to the expiration or termination of the probation period."[40] Once a period of probation expires, the court generally loses jurisdiction over the defendant, except as described below.[41]

B. Hearings after Expiration

The main exception to the jurisdictional rule described above is set out in G.S. 15A-1344(f), which grants a court jurisdiction to hear probation matters after a period of probation has expired if a violation report is filed before expiration. This extended jurisdiction becomes important when, for example, an alleged violation occurs near the end of a period of probation and the hearing cannot be held before it expires.

Under G.S. 15A-1344(f), the court may extend, modify, or revoke probation after the expiration of the period of probation if all the following apply:

1. The State files a written violation report before the expiration of the probation period indicating its intent to conduct a hearing on one or more conditions of probation.
2. The court finds that the probationer violated one or more conditions of probation prior to the expiration of the period of probation.
3. The court finds for good cause shown and stated that probation should be extended, modified, or revoked.[42]

---

39. G.S. 15A-837.
40. G.S. 15A-1344(d).
41. State v. Camp, 229 N.C. 524 (1980).
42. G.S. 15A-1344(f).

To be considered "filed," a violation report should be *file stamped* by the clerk before the probation period expires.[43] In the absence of a file-stamped motion dated before the expiration of probation (or some other evidence proving beyond a reasonable doubt that a violation report was timely filed), the trial court is without jurisdiction to conduct a probation violation hearing after the end of the probationary period. The appellate courts have been demanding in terms of what evidence, aside from a file stamp, suffices to establish beyond a reasonable doubt that a report was timely filed. For example, a report signed and dated by a deputy clerk of superior court was insufficient when the report was not filed stamped.[44]

As to the requirement of "good cause" to act after expiration, the appellate courts have not required a trial judge to make specific written or oral findings supporting a decision that probation should be extended, modified, or revoked. Rather, they have deemed a finding of violation, standing alone, as a sufficient demonstration of the court's consideration of the evidence and determination that good cause existed to act on it.[45]

These jurisdictional provisions apply with equal force to supervised and unsupervised probationers, and to those on probation under G.S. 90-96.[46] The provisions likely also apply in deferred prosecution cases, although no appellate case says so. Generally, upon expiration or early termination of a period of probation imposed as part of a deferred prosecution, the defendant is immune from prosecution on the charges deferred.[47]

The filing of a violation report before a period of probation expires does not itself extend the period of probation beyond the scheduled expiration date. Rather, it merely preserves the court's authority to act on the case at a later hearing. Probation supervision (including the accrual of supervision fees, if any) should cease on the date of expiration unless the court has taken separate action to extend the case.

If a period of probation expires before a probation violation report is filed, the trial court lacks subject matter jurisdiction over the case. Similarly, if an earlier extension of probation was improper and the period of probation would have expired but for the improper extension, the court loses authority to act on the case.[48] The timely filing of one alleged probation violation does not preserve the court's authority to act on additional violations filed after a period of probation has expired. In other words, amendments or addenda to a violation report must themselves comply with the jurisdictional requirements of G.S. 15A-1344(f) (filing before expiration) in order for the court to act on them.

---

43. State v. Hicks, 148 N.C. App. 203 (2001); State v. Moore, 148 N.C. App. 568 (2002).
44. State v. High, 230 N.C. App. 330 (2013).
45. State v. Morgan, ___ N.C. App. ___, 814 S.E.2d 843 (2018); State v. Regan, ___ N.C. App. ___, 800 S.E.2d 436 (2017).
46. State v. Burns, 171 N.C. App. 759 (2005).
47. G.S. 15A-1342(i).
48. State v. Gorman, 221 N.C. App. 330 (2012); State v. Satanek, 190 N.C. App. 653 (2008); State v. Reinhardt, 183 N.C. App. 291 (2007).

Though no statute expressly says so, it is clear that conduct may be considered as a violation only if it occurred while the offender was actually on probation. Thus, when a person commits Crime A before being placed on probation for Crime B, but is convicted of Crime A after being placed on probation for Crime B, the conviction is not a violation of the probation for Crime B.[49]

C. Tolling

Tolling in the probation context means that no time runs off the probationer's period of probation while he or she has a criminal charge pending. In 2011, the General Assembly repealed the tolling law for persons placed on probation on or after December 1, 2011.[50] There are still, however, a small number of probationers who were placed on probation before that date and who are thus subject to the law that existed beforehand, described below.

The tolling statute, originally set out in G.S. 15A-1344(d), provided that "[i]f there are pending criminal charges against the probationer in any court of competent jurisdiction, which, upon conviction, could result in revocation proceedings against the probationer for violation of the terms of this probation, the probation period shall be tolled until all pending criminal charges are resolved." As interpreted by the court of appeals, the tolling provision automatically suspended a defendant's probationary period when new criminal charges were brought.[51] Thus, when a probationer was charged for any offense other than a Class 3 misdemeanor (which cannot result in revocation even upon conviction), time stopped running on his or her period of probation immediately and did not start running again until the charge was resolved by way of acquittal, dismissal, or conviction.

In 2009 the General Assembly made several changes to the tolling law.[52] First, the law was moved from G.S. 15A-1344(d) to G.S. 15A-1344(g). Second, the law was amended to make clear that a probationer remained subject to the conditions of probation, including supervision fees, during the tolled period. Third, the law provided that if a probationer whose case was tolled for a new charge was acquitted or had the charge dismissed, he or she would receive credit against the probation period for the time spent under supervision in tolled status. Those provisions applied to "offenses committed" on or after December 1, 2009, which probably was meant to refer to the date of the offense for which the offender was on probation, not the date of the alleged offense that led to the new criminal charge.[53]

The effective date of the 2009 changes to the tolling law left nothing of G.S. 15A-1344(d) for defendants placed on probation before December 1, 2011, for offenses commit-

---

49. *See, e.g.*, United States v. Drinkall, 749 F.2d 20 (8th Cir. 1984).
50. North Carolina Session Law (hereinafter S.L.) 2011-62.
51. State v. Henderson, 179 N.C. App. 191, 195 (2006); *see also* State v. Patterson, 190 N.C. App. 193 (2008).
52. S.L. 2009-372.
53. *Id.* § 11(b).

ted before December 1, 2009, who are brought to court for a violation hearing on or after December 1, 2009. The legislation removed the original tolling provision in G.S. 15A-1344(d) from the law, effective for "hearings held on or after December 1, 2009."[54] As a result, a trial court lacks jurisdiction to hold a violation hearing on a probationer whose case is tolled under G.S. 15A-1344(d) (assuming the probation period would have expired but for the tolling), because holding the hearing triggers the effective date and negates the effect of the tolling itself.[55] In early 2015, many probationers and inmates affected by the court of appeals decision in *State v. Sitosky* successfully challenged their continued supervision or incarceration.

D. Preliminary Violation Hearings

Under G.S. 15A-1345(c), the court must hold a preliminary hearing on a probation violation within 7 working days of an arrest, unless the probationer waives the preliminary hearing or a final violation hearing is held first. The purpose of the preliminary hearing is to determine whether there is probable cause to believe that the probationer violated a condition of probation. If the hearing is not held, the probationer must be released 7 working days after his or her arrest to continue on probation pending a hearing, unless the probationer is covered under G.S. 15A-1345(b1) and has been determined to be a danger to the public, in which case he or she must be held until the final revocation hearing.[56] The release does not dismiss the violation; rather, it just means that the probationer cannot be detained any longer without a hearing.

The preliminary hearing should be conducted by a judge sitting in the county where the probationer was arrested or the alleged violation occurred.[57] If no judge is sitting in the county where the hearing would otherwise be held, the hearing may be held anywhere in the district.[58] No statutory language limits authority to conduct a preliminary hearing to a judge entitled to sit in the court which imposed probation (as is the case in G.S. 15A-1344(a), limiting the ultimate authority to alter or revoke probation). Thus, apparently any judge—district or superior court—may conduct the preliminary hearing, regardless of which court imposed the probation. That makes sense as a practical matter, as superior court may not be in session within 7 working days of an alleged violation in many districts in North Carolina.

A preliminary hearing must be held only when the probationer is detained for a violation of probation; it is not required when the probationer is released on bail pending the final violation hearing.[59] A failure to hold a preliminary hearing does not deprive the court of jurisdiction to conduct a final violation hearing.[60]

---

54. *Id.* § 11(a).
55. State v. Sitosky, 238 N.C. App. 558 (2014).
56. *See supra* note 33 and accompanying text.
57. G.S. 15A-1345(d).
58. *Id.*
59. State v. O'Connor, 31 N.C. App. 518 (1976).
60. State v. Seay, 59 N.C. App. 667 (1982).

The State must give the probationer notice of the preliminary hearing and its purpose, including a statement of the violations alleged. At the hearing, the probationer may appear and speak in his or her own behalf, may present relevant information, and may, on request, personally question adverse informants unless the court finds good cause for not allowing confrontation. Formal rules of evidence do not apply.[61]

Regarding the right to counsel, the statutory subsection setting out the procedure applicable at a preliminary hearing, G.S. 15A-1345(d), is silent. By contrast, the statute applicable to final violation hearings (G.S. 15A-1345(e)) expressly notes an entitlement to counsel, including appointed counsel if the defendant is indigent. Nevertheless, G.S. 7A-451(a)(4) states that an indigent person is entitled to counsel at "a hearing for revocation of probation," which arguably refers to both preliminary and final violation hearings. Notwithstanding the ambiguity in the statutes, many probationers have a constitutional right to counsel at the preliminary hearing—including any probationer who denies the alleged violation.[62]

If probable cause is found at the preliminary hearing (or if the hearing is waived), the probationer may be detained for a final violation hearing. If probable cause is not found, the probationer must be released to continue on probation.

E. Final Violation Hearings

1. Proper Court and Venue

Any judge of the same level (district or superior court) as the sentencing judge, located in the district where (a) the probation was imposed, (b) the alleged violation took place, or (c) the probationer currently resides, has authority to reduce, modify, extend, continue, terminate, or revoke probation.[63] When a probation judgment is subsequently modified, the court in which the modification occurred is considered to have "imposed" the modification within the language of G.S. 15A-1344(a), and is thus also a proper venue for a violation hearing.[64]

A judge who sentences a defendant to unsupervised probation may limit jurisdiction to alter or revoke the probation to him- or herself.[65] If the sentencing judge does so, the probation may be reduced, terminated, continued, extended, modified, or revoked only by the sentencing judge or, if the sentencing judge is no longer on the

---

61. G.S. 15A-1345(d).

62. *See* Gagnon v. Scarpelli, 411 U.S. 778, 790 (1973) (holding that an indigent defendant has a right to appointed counsel at both the preliminary and final violation hearing in the following circumstances: when he or she denies the alleged violation, in cases where there are substantial reasons which justified or mitigated the violation and those reasons are complex or otherwise difficult to develop or present, and in cases where the probationer may have difficulty speaking effectively for him- or herself).

63. G.S. 15A-1344(a).

64. State v. Mauck, 204 N.C. App. 583 (2010).

65. G.S. 15A-1342(h).

bench, by a presiding judge in the court where the defendant was sentenced.[66] There is no comparable provision for supervised probation.

Some additional rules apply when probation matters arise in places other than the district in which the probation was initially imposed. First, a court may always on its own motion return a probationer for hearing to the district where probation was imposed or the district where the probationer resides.[67] Second, the district attorney of the prosecutorial district in which probation was imposed must be given reasonable notice of any hearing that will "affect probation substantially."[68] Third, if a judge reduces, terminates, extends, modifies, or revokes probation outside the county where the judgment was entered, the clerk of court must send a copy of that judge's order and any other records to the court where probation was originally imposed. If probation is revoked, the clerk in the county of revocation issues the commitment order.[69]

For defendants on probation as part of a deferred prosecution or conditional discharge, violations are reported to the court and to the district attorney in the district where the case originated.[70] For a variety of reasons, it makes sense for violation hearings in those cases to be handled in the district of origin.[71]

Class H and I felonies pled in district court. Under G.S. 7A-272(c), with the consent of the presiding district court judge, the prosecutor, and the defendant, the district court has jurisdiction to accept a plea of guilty or no contest to a Class H or I felony. If a person enters a felony plea in district court, is placed on probation, and is later alleged to have violated that probation, the violation hearing is, by default, held in superior court. The district court can hold the violation hearing if the State and the defendant consent (consent of the judge is not required under the statute).[72] Appeal of a violation hearing held in district court is to superior court for a de novo hearing, not to the court of appeals.[73]

Supervision of felony drug treatment court or a therapeutic court in district court. With the consent of the chief district court judge and the senior resident superior court judge, the district court has jurisdiction to preside over the supervision of a probation judgment entered in superior court in which the defendant is required to participate in a drug treatment court program or a therapeutic court.[74] In cases where the requisite judges give their consent, a district court judge may modify or extend probation judgments supervised under G.S. 7A-272(e). The superior court has exclusive jurisdiction to revoke probation of cases supervised under G.S. 7A-272(e), except

---

66. G.S. 15A-1344(b).
67. G.S. 15A-1344(c).
68. G.S. 15A-1344(a).
69. G.S. 15A-1344(c).
70. G.S. 15A-1342(a1).
71. *See infra* notes 189–193 and accompanying text.
72. G.S. 7A-271(e).
73. State v. Hooper, 358 N.C. 122 (2004).
74. A therapeutic court is one that promotes activities designed to address underlying problems of substance abuse and mental illness that contribute to a person's criminal activity. G.S. 7A-272(e).

that the district court has jurisdiction to conduct the revocation proceeding when the chief district court judge and the senior resident superior court judge agree that it is in the interest of justice that the proceedings be conducted by the district court.[75] Unlike non–drug treatment court cases, however, if the district court exercises jurisdiction to revoke probation in a case supervised under G.S. 7A-272(e), appeal of an order revoking probation is to the appellate division, not to superior court.[76]

2. Hearing Procedure

A probation violation hearing is not a criminal prosecution or a formal trial.[77] Nevertheless, certain procedural requirements apply as a matter of statute and constitutional due process. At the hearing, evidence against the probationer must be disclosed to him or her, and the probationer may appear, speak, and present relevant information.[78] The defendant is entitled to a written statement from the court as to the evidence relied on and reasons for revoking probation,[79] but apparently no verbatim transcript is required.[80]

Confrontation. The probationer may confront and cross-examine witnesses unless the court finds good cause for not allowing confrontation.[81] Confrontation in this context is a due process right, not a Sixth Amendment right under the Confrontation Clause.[82] If the court disallows confrontation, it must make findings that there was good cause for doing so. In *State v. Coltrane*, for example, the supreme court reversed a probation revocation when the trial court did not allow the probationer to confront her probation officer (who was not present at the hearing) without making findings of good cause for not allowing confrontation.[83]

Right to counsel. The defendant has a clear statutory right to counsel at the final violation hearing, including appointed counsel if indigent.[84]

The court must comply with G.S. 15A-1242 when accepting a waiver of the right to counsel at a probation violation hearing, just as it must at trial.[85] The court must inquire whether the defendant (1) has been clearly advised of his or her right to counsel, (2) understands the consequences of a decision to proceed without counsel, and (3) comprehends the nature of the charges and the range of permissible punishments. It is unclear whether a waiver of counsel taken at a preliminary hearing is valid for the

---

75. G.S. 7A-271(f).

76. *Id.*

77. State v. Duncan, 270 N.C. 241 (1967); State v. Pratt, 21 N.C. App. 538 (1974).

78. G.S. 15A-1345(e).

79. Morrissey v. Brewer, 408 U.S. 471 (1972).

80. *See* State v. Quick, 179 N.C. App. 647 (2006) (affirming a probation revocation despite the notes and transcript of the revocation hearing being misplaced; the defendant was unable to demonstrate any prejudice resulting from the missing record).

81. G.S. 15A-1345(e).

82. State v. Braswell, 283 N.C. 332 (1973).

83. 307 N.C. 511 (1983).

84. G.S. 15A-1345(e).

85. State v. Evans, 153 N.C. App. 313 (2002).

final violation hearing as well. There is authority to suggest that it is,[86] but the better practice is to conduct the waiver colloquy again before the final violation hearing.

Evidence. The rules of evidence do not apply at probation violation hearings.[87] There is thus no statutory rule against admitting hearsay at the hearing. Older appellate cases held that hearsay alone was insufficient to support a revocation of probation,[88] but more recent cases appear to have relaxed that rule. In *State v. Murchison*, for example, the defendant was revoked based on hearsay testimony (a statement by the defendant's mother to the probation officer) that he had violated his probation by committing a new criminal offense.[89] The record or recollection of evidence or testimony introduced at the preliminary hearing is inadmissible as evidence at the final violation hearing.[90]

The exclusionary rule also does not apply at probation revocation hearings.[91]

Standard of proof. To activate a suspended sentence for failure to comply with a probation condition, the State must present evidence sufficient to *reasonably satisfy* the judge that the defendant has willfully violated a valid condition of probation or has violated a condition without lawful excuse.[92] Proof to a jury is not required, nor must the proof of the violation be made beyond a reasonable doubt.[93]

When the alleged violation is a failure to satisfy a monetary obligation or a requirement to complete community service, and the probation officer has set the schedule for paying the money or completing the service hours, the State must introduce evidence of those schedules before the judge can make a determination that the defendant has violated them.[94]

Admitted violations. A defendant does not plead "guilty" or "not guilty" to a probation violation. Rather, he or she admits or denies the violation.[95] When a defendant admits to a violation, there is no requirement that the court personally examine him or her pursuant to G.S. 15A-1022 (unlike when a defendant pleads guilty to a criminal charge).[96] A defendant is not entitled to a continuance under G.S. 15A-1023 on matters related to probation when a trial judge rejects a plea bargain in a new criminal case that includes an agreement to continue the defendant on probation in a prior case.[97]

---

86. State v. Kinlock, 152 N.C. App. 84, 88–89 (2002).

87. G.S. 15A-1345(e); G.S. 8C-1, Art. 11, R. 1101, § (b)(3).

88. *See* State v. Hewett, 270 N.C. 348, 356 (1967) (noting that some of the trial judge's findings of fact were based on hearsay evidence that "should not have been considered by the judge" but upholding the judge's revocation order based on other evidence); State v. Pratt, 21 N.C. App. 538 (1974).

89. 367 N.C. 461 (2014).

90. G.S. 15A-1345(e).

91. State v. Lombardo, 74 N.C. App. 460 (1985).

92. State v. Duncan, 270 N.C. 241 (1967); State v. White, 129 N.C. App. 52 (1998).

93. State v. Freeman, 47 N.C. App. 171 (1980).

94. State v. Boone, 225 N.C. App. 423, 425 (2013) ("[The probation officer's] conclusory testimony that defendant was in arrears is insufficient to support a finding that defendant had willfully violated the terms of his probation by failing to pay the required fees or perform community service on time.").

95. State v. Sellers, 185 N.C. App. 726 (2007).

96. *Id.*

97. State v. Cleary, 213 N.C. App. 198 (2011).

IV. Probation Response Options

At the conclusion of a proper hearing (or once the defendant has waived his or her right to a hearing), the court may take one or more of the actions described below. The options are arranged roughly from most restrictive to least restrictive, from the standpoint of the defendant. The table on the inside front cover of this booklet summarizes the available options.

In many instances, the response options are not mutually exclusive. For instance, the court may impose a split sentence, extend the period of probation, and otherwise modify the conditions of probation all in response to a single violation. In general, changes to probation short of revocation are ordered using Form AOC-CR-609, *Order on Violation of Probation or on Motion to Modify*. A judgment and commitment upon revocation of probation is entered on Form AOC-CR-607 for a felony, Form AOC-CR-608 for a misdemeanor, and Form AOC-CR-343 for impaired driving.[98] Modifications and dispositions in deferred prosecution cases are entered on Form AOC-CR-634. In conditional discharge cases, use Form AOC-CR-635.

Except as otherwise indicated, the court has broad discretion when crafting the appropriate response to a violation of probation—including the discretion to take no action at all. When a person has committed multiple violations, the court can choose which of them, if any, to respond to. And when a person is on probation for multiple crimes, the court may take the same or different actions in each case. Regardless of the number and type of prior violations, the court is never required to revoke a person's probation.

A. Revocation

Revocation means the probationer's suspended sentence is activated and the probationer is ordered to jail or prison. Prior to the Justice Reinvestment Act of 2011, the longstanding rule in North Carolina was that any single violation of a valid probation condition was a sufficient basis for revocation.[99] For violations occurring on or after December 1, 2011, however, the court's authority to revoke probation is substantially

---

98. Court officials should be aware that probation officers are guided by an administrative policy that directs how they respond to perceived violations of probation. The policy includes a chart that directs different types of responses depending on the type of violation at issue and the offender's supervision level. For example, nonrecurring violations by low-risk offenders should be responded to with a modest intervention, such as a reprimand or an additional contact by a probation officer, while new crimes or other violations implicating public safety will lead to the issuance of a probation violation report and the arrest of the probationer. *See* Markham, *supra* note 5, at 49–51 (summarizing the policy set out in Community Corrections Policy, *supra* note 24, at § D.0202). That administrative policy is not binding on the courts, but it helps explain which offenders probation officers bring back before the court for a hearing and the types of actions officers recommend to the court.

99. *See, e.g.*, State v. Tozzi, 84 N.C. App. 517 (1987).

limited. For those violations, the court may only revoke probation in the first instance for either of the following:

- violations of the **commit no criminal offense** condition set out in G.S. 15A-1343(b)(1) (hereinafter "new criminal offense" violations), although not solely a conviction for a Class 3 misdemeanor; or
- violations of the statutory **absconding** condition set out in G.S. 15A-1343(b)(3a).

For violations aside from new criminal offenses and absconding (hereinafter "technical violations"), a probationer can be revoked only if he or she has committed two previous technical violations that have been responded to in a specific way, which varies depending on the type of case and when the person was placed on probation:

- **Felony** probationers may be revoked for any violation after receiving two 90-day periods of confinement in response to violation (CRV).
- **Impaired driving (DWI)** probationers may be revoked for any violation after receiving two periods of CRV of up to 90 days each.
- **Misdemeanor probationers placed on probation on or after December 1, 2015**, may be revoked for any violation after previously receiving at least two periods of 2- or 3-day quick-dip confinement, imposed either by a judge or by a probation officer through delegated authority, in response to a technical violation.
- **Misdemeanor probationers placed on probation before December 1, 2015**, are still subject to old law that says they may be revoked for any violation after previously receiving at least two periods of CRV of up to 90 days each.

With these requirements in place, the probation law takes a "three strikes" approach to technical violations: a person may not be revoked until his or her third "strike." As to strikes one and two, only the specific sanctions noted above—CRV or a quick dip, as the case may be—qualify as strikes. Thus, it is the prior *sanction*, not the prior violation itself, that puts the person on a path to revocation, and violations responded to in some other way (by a term of special probation or electronic house arrest, for example) do not count as strikes. Additional details about CRV and quick dips are set out below.[100]

---

100. *See infra* notes 135–159 and accompanying text.

REVOCATION

CONFINEMENT IN RESPONSE TO VIOLATION (CRV)

QUICK DIP

SPECIAL PROBATION (SPLIT)

CONTEMPT

EXTENSION

MODIFICATION

TRANSFER TO UNSUPERVISED PROBATION

TERMINATION

CONTINUATION WITHOUT MODIFICATION

Grounds for Revocation:
New criminal offense or absconding

Revocation Eligibility for a Technical Violation:

Felons—after two prior CRVs (90 days each)

DWI—after two prior CRVs (up to 90 days each)

Misdemeanors—

Placed on probation on or after December 1, 2015: After two prior quick dips (2–3 days each), imposed by a judge or by a probation officer

Placed on probation before December 1, 2015: After two prior CRVs (up to 90 days each)

In general, an activated sentence commences on the day probation is revoked,[101] although a court may probably delay service of the sentence to some future date in its order revoking probation.[102] A judge also apparently may stay execution of an order revoking probation until some future date, allowing the defendant a final opportunity to comply with his or her conditions in the meantime.[103] For crimes sentenced under Structured Sentencing, an activated sentence must be served in a continuous block; the court may not order it served in noncontinuous intervals.[104] Active sentences for impaired driving may be served on weekends.[105]

1. Changes to a Sentence upon Revocation

Generally a sentence is activated in the same form in which it was entered by the original sentencing judge, with the defendant committed to the custodian identified in the judgment suspending sentence. However, the revoking judge has limited discretion to modify the sentence, as described below.

Reduction of the suspended sentence. A revoking court can, upon revocation, reduce the length of a suspended sentence of imprisonment. For felonies, the reduction must be within the original range (presumptive, mitigated, or aggravated) established for the class of offense and prior record level of the sentence being activated. For misdemeanors, the sentence may be reduced to as little as one day upon revocation, because that is the shortest permissible sentence in every cell on the misdemeanor sentencing grid.[106] The court may reduce a sentence only at the point of revocation.[107]

Consecutive and concurrent sentences upon revocation. Under G.S. 15A-1344(d), a "sentence activated upon revocation of probation commences on the day probation is revoked and runs concurrently with any other period of probation, parole, or imprisonment to which the defendant is subject during that period *unless the revoking judge specifies that it is to run consecutively with the other period.*" The court of appeals has interpreted the last clause of that provision to mean that the revoking judge can change the concurrent or consecutive decision rendered by the original sentencing judge, allowing sentences initially ordered to run consecutively to run

---

101. *Id.*

102. G.S. 15A-1353(a). *See* Official Commentary to G.S. 15A-1353, providing that subsection (a) of the law "applies both to an initial sentence to imprisonment and to the activation of a sentence following probation revocation." The commentary goes on to say that while the "presumptive beginning date for the term of imprisonment is the date of the commitment order, the judge may specify a delayed beginning dated to permit the defendant to get his affairs in order."

103. State v. Yonce, 207 N.C. App. 658 (2010) (approving a trial judge's order staying a defendant's revocation of probation to allow the probationer additional time to pay restitution).

104. State v. Miller, 205 N.C. App. 291 (2010).

105. G.S. 20-179(s) ("The judge in his discretion may order a term of imprisonment to be served on weekends.").

106. G.S. 15A-1344(d1).

107. State v. Mills, 86 N.C. App. 479 (1987).

concurrently,[108] or vice-versa.[109] The judge may also run an activated sentence consecutive to a later-arising active sentence, even though the later sentence was for an offense that occurred after the original probationary judgment was entered.[110] If the revoking judge does not specifically state on the judgment activating the suspended sentence that it is to run consecutively to another sentence, the Division of Adult Correction and Juvenile Justice will run the activated sentence concurrently with any other sentence the defendant is obligated to serve.

There is no authority to *consolidate* activated sentences with newly imposed judgments, as the statutes governing consolidation apply only to defendants convicted of more than one offense at the same time.[111]

2. Revocation-Eligible Violations

Each type of revocation-eligible violation (a new criminal offense, absconding, or a technical violation after two previous CRV periods or quick dips) raises complicated issues, explored below.

New criminal offense. It is a regular condition of probation that a probationer "[c]ommit no criminal offense in any jurisdiction."[112] The court may revoke probation upon a first violation of the condition.[113]

A common question related to the new criminal offense condition is whether a person must be convicted of the new crime before the court may find it as a violation of probation, or whether a pending charge (or even uncharged or acquitted conduct) could constitute a "criminal offense" within its meaning. The cases make clear that the defendant need not be convicted of the new criminal conduct before the court may respond to it as a probation violation. A finding of violation is proper either if the defendant has been convicted,[114] or if the probation court makes an independent finding that the alleged criminal act occurred.[115] That finding must, however, be based on evidence presented at the violation hearing (or the defendant's admission), not on the mere fact that a charge is pending.

---

108. State v. Hanner, 188 N.C. App. 137 (2008); State v. Paige, 90 N.C. App. 142 (1988).

109. The original judgment in *Hanner* was part of a plea arrangement, though it appears that the original sentencing court ran certain sentences concurrently even though the defendant had actually agreed as part of the plea that they would run *consecutively*. Thus, when the revoking judge eventually ran the sentences consecutively, he did not do anything that the defendant had not agreed to in the initial plea arrangement. As a result, *Hanner* probably should not be viewed as strong authority for the idea that a revoking judge can disregard the terms of a plea arrangement calling for concurrent sentences and impose consecutive sentences upon revocation of probation.

110. State v. Campbell, 90 N.C. App. 761 (1988).

111. G.S. 15A-1340.15(b) (consolidation of felonies); -1340.22(b) (consolidation of misdemeanors).

112. G.S. 15A-1343(b)(1).

113. G.S. 15A-1344(a).

114. State v. Guffey, 253 N.C. 43 (1960).

115. State v. Monroe, 83 N.C. App. 143, 145 (1986) ("All that is required in revoking a suspended sentence is evidence which reasonably satisfies the judge in the use of his sound discretion that a condition of probation has been willfully violated.").

REVOCATION

CONFINEMENT IN RESPONSE TO VIOLATION (CRV)

QUICK DIP

SPECIAL PROBATION (SPLIT)

CONTEMPT

EXTENSION

MODIFICATION

TRANSFER TO UNSUPERVISED PROBATION

TERMINATION

CONTINUATION WITHOUT MODIFICATION

Additionally, it is apparently permissible for a probation court to find that a probationer has committed a new criminal offense regardless of the State's decision to drop the new criminal charge[116] or to not bring a charge at all.[117] There is also support for the idea that the probation court may revoke probation based on its own independent findings of a criminal act even if the defendant is acquitted of the new criminal charge,[118] but the appellate courts describe this as against the better practice.[119] Revocation in lieu of, or even in addition to, a new criminal conviction does not constitute double jeopardy; the probation revocation is not new punishment for the same act but is, rather, the activation of a punishment previously imposed for conviction of a prior crime.[120]

Just because a probation court may find a violation based on unconvicted conduct does not mean it must. In many districts in North Carolina, it is common practice to await the resolution of a pending charge before responding to it in probation court, treating it as a new criminal offense violation only if the defendant is convicted. Probation policy directs officers to consult with their chief probation parole officer and the district attorney when a probationer is charged with a new crime, and leaves it to the district attorney to decide whether to proceed with a probation violation hearing before the defendant is convicted on the new charge.[121]

If the violation hearing is held first, and a violation is found, a court later considering the criminal charge probably is not bound by that finding at trial. The defendant is of course entitled to proof beyond a reasonable doubt on the criminal charge, and the finding of a probation violation—with its lower standard of proof, and with fewer procedural protections—would not have preclusive effect.[122] If no violation is found, it is unclear whether that determination would be binding in a subsequent trial.[123]

---

116. *See* State v. Debnam, 23 N.C. App. 478 (1974) (upholding the trial court's revocation based on a nolle prossed charge).

117. *Monroe*, 83 N.C. App. at 145–46.

118. *See* State v. Greer, 173 N.C. 759 (1917) (holding that a jury verdict acquitting the defendant of a new criminal charge was not binding on the probation court so long as the court found facts based on the evidence before it).

119. *See Debnam*, 23 N.C. App. at 481 ("It may not be desirable for a judge to activate a suspended sentence upon conduct where a jury has found the defendant not guilty of a charge arising out of that conduct, but it appears to be within the power of the judge to do so.").

120. State v. Sparks, 362 N.C. 181 (2008); State v. Monk, 132 N.C. App. 248 (1999).

121. Community Corrections Policy, *supra* note 24, at § D.0204(a).

122. *See, e.g.*, State v. Byrd, 58 P.3d 50, 58 (Colo. 2002) (holding that, despite an identity of issues and parties, the violation hearing was not a "full and fair opportunity to litigate the issue" sufficient for collateral estoppel to apply at a subsequent trial related to the same criminal behavior).

123. *Cf.* State v. Summers, 315 N.C. 620 (2000) (holding that collateral estoppel barred relitigation at a DWI trial of a prior superior court finding, made at an appeal of a DMV license revocation, that the defendant did not willfully refuse a chemical analysis. Courts in other jurisdictions that have considered the question have generally declined to give probation findings preclusive effect at a subsequent trial. *See, e.g.*, Lucido v. Superior Court, 795 P.2d 1223 (1990) ("Because public policy requires that ultimate determinations of criminal guilt and innocence not be made at probation revocation hearings, barring relitigation of issues at trial will not preserve the integrity of the judicial system.").

Sometimes—either pursuant to a plea agreement or in the judge's own discretion—the court sentencing a new conviction will order that the new conviction not violate the defendant's existing probation. There is no statute approving such orders, and as a technical matter the court sentencing the new conviction has jurisdiction over the probation matter only if a violation report has been filed before the same court. As a practical matter, though, such orders are often honored—either because the defendant's guilty plea in the new case was secured pursuant to an agreement that probation would not be revoked, or simply as a matter of comity between judges.

Class 3 misdemeanors. The court may not revoke a defendant's probation solely for conviction of a Class 3 misdemeanor.[124] That prohibition—which predates the Justice Reinvestment Act—operates as an exception to the general rule that probation may be revoked for a new criminal offense. Interpretations of the law vary. Some argue that revocation is permissible when a probationer is convicted of multiple Class 3 misdemeanors, or of a Class 3 misdemeanor and additional technical violations, on the theory that revocation in those instances would not be "solely" for a single Class 3 misdemeanor. Others take the view that multiple violations ineligible for revocation on their own do not accumulate to allow for revocation. The appellate courts have yet to consider the question in a published case.

Regardless of the answer to that question, courts should bear in mind that a conviction for a Class 3 misdemeanor is still a violation of the "commit no criminal offense" condition and therefore not a "technical violation." That leaves a Class 3 misdemeanor in the unusual position of being ineligible for revocation, but also ineligible for CRV (which, the statute says, is expressly for violations other than a new criminal offense or absconding).

Absconding. For probation violations occurring on or after December 1, 2011, the court may revoke probation for a violation of the statutory absconding condition set out in G.S. 15A-1343(b)(3a). That subsection provides that a probationer may not "abscond, by willfully avoiding supervision or by willfully making the defendant's whereabouts unknown to the supervising probation officer."

The absconding condition was created as part of the Justice Reinvestment Act and applies only to defendants on probation for offenses committed on or after December 1, 2011.[125] By now, most probationers are on probation for offenses committed after that date. Those under supervision for older offenses are not subject to the revocation-eligible absconding condition, and violations of other conditions (such as the "remain within the jurisdiction" condition or the "failure to report to the officer" condition) are ineligible for revocation, even if probation officers refer to them as absconding.[126] If a probationer actually absconded before December 1, 2011, that offending behavior would be eligible for revocation because it predates the effective date of the JRA's limitation on revocation authority. The court of appeals has referred to the gap

REVOCATION
CONFINEMENT IN RESPONSE TO VIOLATION (CRV)
QUICK DIP
SPECIAL PROBATION (SPLIT)
CONTEMPT
EXTENSION
MODIFICATION
TRANSFER TO UNSUPERVISED PROBATION
TERMINATION
CONTINUATION WITHOUT MODIFICATION

---

124. G.S. 15A-1344(d).
125. S.L. 2011-412, § 2.5.
126. State v. Nolen, 228 N.C. App. 203 (2013).

period affecting probationers on probation for offenses committed before December 1, 2011, who absconded on or after that date as a "donut hole" in the absconding law.[127]

Even for offenders actually subject to the statutory absconding condition, the language of the condition itself does not define "avoiding supervision" or state how long a person's whereabouts must be unknown before he or she becomes an absconder. At one end of the spectrum, a probationer does not become an absconder by missing one office appointment the day after seeing his probation officer.[128] At the other end of the spectrum, a probationer who changed address without permission and made his whereabouts unknown to probation officers for several months was properly deemed an absconder.[129]

In between those extremes, whether a probationer has violated the absconding condition appears to be a fairly fact-specific inquiry. In *State v. Williams*, for example, the court of appeals concluded that a defendant who missed multiple office visits over a three-month period and traveled to New Jersey without permission was not an absconder. The absconding allegations were, the court held, "simply a re-alleging" of the technical violations of failing to report to the probation officer and failing to remain within the jurisdiction.[130] The court also appeared to find it significant that the probationer's whereabouts were not unknown, because he told his probation officer over the phone that he was in New Jersey. In *State v. Melton*, the court of appeals held there was insufficient evidence of absconding when "the probation officer is unable to reach a defendant after merely two days of attempts, only leaving messages with a defendant's relatives."[131] In *State v. Krider*, there was insufficient evidence of absconding when the State failed to establish the identity of a witness who told the supervising officer that the probationer no longer lived at the designated residence.[132]

Probation officers are required as a matter of their own policy to conduct a specialized investigation before declaring that an offender has absconded. That investigation includes attempting to contact the offender by telephone, visiting the offender's residence in the daytime and in the evening, contacting the offender's landlord and neighbors, visiting the offender's workplace or school, contacting the offender's relatives and associates, and contacting local law enforcement, including the jail.[133] Officers alleging absconding violations appear to be on the strongest legal footing when they include the details of this investigation in their violation report, especially those details that exceed the technical violations of failing to report or leaving North Carolina.

Probationers alleged to have absconded are still subject to the jurisdictional provisions of G.S. 15A-1344(f) regarding violation hearings held after the expiration of the

---

127. State v. Johnson, ___ N.C. App. ___, 803 S.E.2d 827 (2017).
128. State v. Johnson, 246 N.C. App. 139 (2016).
129. State v. Johnson, 246 N.C. App. 132 (2016).
130. 243 N.C. App. 198 (2015).
131. ___ N.C. App. ___, 811 S.E.2d 678 (2018).
132. State v. Krider, ___ N.C. App. ___, 810 S.E.2d 828, *aff'd*, ___ N.C. ___, ___ S.E.2d ___ (Sept. 21, 2018).
133. *See* COMMUNITY CORRECTIONS POLICY, *supra* note 24, at § D.0503.

probationary period.[134] Thus, even if a probationer has clearly made him- or herself unavailable for supervision, the probation officer must file a violation report before the case expires to preserve the court's power to act if the probationer is eventually apprehended.

REVOCATION

CONFINEMENT IN RESPONSE TO VIOLATION (CRV)

QUICK DIP

SPECIAL PROBATION (SPLIT)

CONTEMPT

EXTENSION

MODIFICATION

TRANSFER TO UNSUPERVISED PROBATION

TERMINATION

CONTINUATION WITHOUT MODIFICATION

B. Confinement in Response to Violation (CRV)

1. CRV Generally

CRV is a probation sanction permissible in response to technical violations of probation. It is a period of imprisonment, generally shorter than a full revocation of probation, created as part of the Justice Reinvestment Act and designed to help reduce the prison population attributable to probationers who commit relatively minor violations. After an eligible probationer has received two CRV periods, he or she may be revoked for any subsequent violation of probation. Initially, CRV was an option for all probationers (felons, misdemeanants, and impaired drivers), but it was repealed as an option for Structured Sentencing misdemeanants placed on probation on or after December 1, 2015.[135]

CRV may be ordered only in response to technical violations of probation—that is, any violation of probation other than a new criminal offense under G.S. 15A-1343(b)(1) or absconding under G.S. 15A-1343(b)(3a).[136] For a new criminal offense or absconding, the court may not impose CRV. Instead, it may either revoke probation or take one of the other actions described below. Under the effective date language of the Justice Reinvestment Act, the court does not have authority to impose CRV for violations that occurred before December 1, 2011.[137]

CRV is never mandatory. For example, the court could impose special probation or electronic house arrest in response to a technical violation—or it could do nothing at all. However, those responses would not count as "strikes," putting the defendant on a path toward eligibility for revocation for a subsequent technical violation.

When a defendant is on probation for multiple offenses, the law requires CRV periods to run concurrently on "all cases related to the violation," and confinement is to be "immediate unless otherwise specified by the court."[138] Together, these statutory rules indicate that multiple CRV periods should not be "stacked" to create a confinement period of longer than 90 days. The statute is silent, however, on the question of whether a CRV period may be run consecutively to other forms of probationary confinement, like special probation.

The court should use a modification order, Form AOC-CR-609, to impose CRV.

---

134. State v. Burns, 171 N.C. App. 759, 762 (2005) ("The mere notation of 'absconder' on the order for arrest did not relieve the State of its duty to make reasonable efforts to notify defendant under [G.S. 15A-1344].").

135. S.L. 2015-191.

136. G.S. 15A-1344(d2).

137. S.L. 2011-192, § 4.(d) ("This section is effective December 1, 2011, and applies to probation violations occurring on or after that date.").

138. G.S. 15A-1344(d2).

Due to a series of legislative revisions between 2011 and today, the technical rules regarding CRV applicability, length, and place of confinement vary depending on the defendant's offense date; date placed on probation; and whether he or she is under supervision for a felony, a misdemeanor sentenced under Structured Sentencing, or impaired driving.

2. Felony CRV

In felony cases, a CRV period is 90 days—no more, no less. The only exception to that rule would be a probationer who has 90 days or less remaining on his or her suspended sentence (unlikely in a felony case), in which case the CRV period is for the remainder of the suspended sentence. The 90 days must be served continuously (the court cannot order them served on weekends, for example), and they must be served in the custody of the Division of Adult Correction and Juvenile Justice.[139] Men ordered to serve CRV are generally housed in one of the state's two CRV centers for men in Robeson County and Burke County, unless the probationer has medical issues or raises security concerns that cannot be addressed in those locations, in which case the time is served in prison. Women generally serve felony CRV at North Piedmont Correctional Institution in Davidson County.

3. CRV for Structured Sentencing Misdemeanors

Whether the court may impose CRV for a misdemeanor sentenced under Structured Sentencing (generally, any crime other than impaired driving and the handful of other offenses sentenced under G.S. 20-179) depends on when the person was placed on probation.

For Structured Sentencing misdemeanants **placed on probation on or after December 1, 2015, CRV is repealed** and therefore unavailable as a response to any probation violation.[140] In those cases, the court may respond to a technical violation with a "quick dip" in the jail (described below) or some other probation response option aside from revocation and CRV.

For misdemeanor defendants placed on probation before December 1, 2015, CRV is still a viable response to a probation violation. For those probationers, CRV is—like felony CRV—permissible for any technical violation, but not in response to a new criminal offense or absconding. The CRV period for any such probationer may be "up to 90 days," meaning the court may impose a period shorter than 90 days in its discretion. Of course, if the defendant's suspended sentence is less than 90 days (as many misdemeanor sentences are), the maximum length of the CRV period is the length of the suspended sentence itself. As with felonies, misdemeanor CRV must be served in a continuous period.

CRV for any misdemeanor probationer is served "where the defendant would have served an active sentence,"[141] which is the place of confinement identified for the

---

139. *Id.*
140. *Id.*; S.L. 2015-191.
141. G.S. 15A-1344(d2).

suspended term of imprisonment in the judgment suspending sentence. For sentences initially imposed on or after January 1, 2015, the place of confinement for a misdemeanor sentence of greater than 90 days will be the Statewide Misdemeanant Confinement Program, while shorter sentences are generally served in the local jail.[142] Different place-of-confinement rules were in effect for defendants initially sentenced before January 1, 2015; therefore, the place of confinement for CRV for those probationers could differ from that which would apply to a defendant sentenced today.

4. CRV for Impaired Drivers

For DWI, CRV of "up to 90 days" is permissible in response to any technical violation.

CRV for impaired drivers is, like CRV for other misdemeanants, served "where the defendant would have served an active sentence."[143] Thus, for sentences initially imposed on or after January 1, 2015, the place of confinement for any CRV for a DWI, regardless of level, will be the Statewide Misdemeanant Confinement Program.[144]

5. Jail Credit Applied to CRV

The rules for applying jail credit to CRV vary depending on the type of crime for which the person is on probation and the date of the alleged violation.

If the court orders felony CRV for a probation violation committed on or after October 1, 2014, it must *not* reduce the 90-day term of CRV for any time already served in the case. Instead, any credit will be applied to the defendant's suspended sentence in the event of revocation.[145] That rule prohibits the application of prehearing confinement or any other form of jail credit (such as pretrial confinement) to a felony CRV period.

For probation violations that occurred before October 1, 2014, the rule for felony CRV was exactly the opposite: If a defendant was detained in advance of a violation hearing at which CRV was ordered, the judge *must* apply that prehearing credit to the CRV period, with any excess time applied to a later-activated sentence.[146] Today there will be few hearings on violations that old, but if one should arise, the court should use the prior law and apply any prehearing credit to the CRV.

For misdemeanor probationers still eligible for CRV and impaired drivers, the General Statutes are silent on the issue of jail credit applied to CRV. The law neither requires nor forbids the credit, giving the trial judge apparent flexibility to apply credit in his or her discretion.

In all cases, before imposing a CRV period, the court should consider whether, in light of the time the defendant has already served in the case, there is enough time remaining on the suspended sentence to cover the length of the CRV period the court wishes to impose. The jail credit rules should not be applied in a way that exposes a defendant to incarceration in excess of his or her maximum sentence.

REVOCATION

CONFINEMENT IN RESPONSE TO VIOLATION (CRV)

QUICK DIP

SPECIAL PROBATION (SPLIT)

CONTEMPT

EXTENSION

MODIFICATION

TRANSFER TO UNSUPERVISED PROBATION

TERMINATION

CONTINUATION WITHOUT MODIFICATION

---

142. G.S. 15A-1352.
143. *Id.*
144. G.S. 15A-1352.
145. G.S. 15A-1344(d2).
146. *Id.*; S.L. 2014-100, § 16C.8.(a).

6. Revocation after Two CRV Periods

A defendant may receive only two CRV periods in a particular probation case. After that, the court may respond to subsequent violations by either revoking probation or imposing some sanction other than CRV.

If a person who previously served CRV later has his or her probation revoked, any time spent imprisoned for CRV must be credited to the defendant's activated sentence.[147] The only exception to that rule is for a probationer on probation for multiple offenses who serves concurrent CRVs for sentences that wind up running consecutively upon revocation. In that situation, credit for the concurrent CRV periods is applied to only one of the defendant's consecutive activated sentences.[148]

7. Terminal CRVs

By design, CRV is a temporary intervention in a probation case—a short period of incarceration in response to a technical violation, followed by a return to probation supervision. In reality, CRV often winds up being the last court action in the case, either because the CRV uses up the entirety of the defendant's suspended sentence, or because the probation period expires while the person is serving the CRV. Both situations are referred to as "terminal CRVs."

The first type of terminal CRV (the type that uses up the entirety of a defendant's suspended sentence) is more likely to occur in the case of a misdemeanor or DWI, where the defendant's suspended sentence could be similar in length to a CRV. A felony maximum sentence, by contrast, will typically exceed 90 days by many months, and so the defendant will likely have ample time remaining on his or her maximum sentence even after serving multiple CRV periods.

Some argue that a felony CRV should nonetheless be considered "terminal" if it carries the defendant past the point where he or she would have been released had the sentence been active. For example, a defendant with a 4–14-month suspended sentence who is serving a second CRV period might argue that he or she should be released from the CRV once he or she has accrued five total months of jail credit on the sentence, as that is the point (the maximum sentence less 9 months) at which he or she would be released from prison to post-release supervision on an active term. However, the rule requiring mandatory release to post-release supervision applies only to felons serving an active sentence.[149] A probationer serving CRV has not been revoked, and so is not serving an "active sentence" within the meaning of the PRS law, and therefore probably should serve the full CRV. A judge wanting to avoid that outcome may wish to impose special probation or some sanction aside from CRV.

As to the second type of terminal CRV (the type where the probation period expires while the defendant is in the midst of the CRV), DACJJ will carry out a court-ordered CRV even if the term of probation has expired. No statute clearly says to do otherwise—unlike the special probation statute, which says that no split

---

147. G.S. 15A-1344(d2); 15-196.1.
148. G.S. 15-196.2.
149. G.S. 15A-1368.1.

sentence may extend beyond the defendant's period of probation.[150] Surprisingly, no appellate case has examined the issue.

A final possibility—officially discouraged by Community Corrections, but nonetheless fairly common—is that the judge will affirmatively terminate the defendant's probation at the conclusion of a CRV period, even when time remains on the suspended sentence and the probation period. This is sometimes referred to as a terminal CRV, but would be better described as a "CRV-and-terminate," to reflect that it is really two orders by the court (a CRV and a termination), and not a single CRV that brings the case to a natural conclusion.

C. "Quick Dip" Confinement

For offenders on probation for Structured Sentencing offenses—felonies or misdemeanors, but not DWI—that occurred on or after December 1, 2011, the court may order jail confinement of 2 or 3 days as a modification of probation. (The choice between 2 or 3 days is in the discretion of the court.) This short term of confinement is sometimes referred to as a "quick dip" in the jail. A defendant may serve no more than 6 days of quick dip confinement per month, and the sanction may be used in no more than 3 separate calendar months of a person's probation.[151] Unlike CRV, which may be imposed only in response to technical violations, the court may impose a quick dip in response to any violation, or even without violation for good cause.[152] Quick dips are always served in a local confinement facility, never in prison. The court may, in its discretion, impose a $40 jail fee for each day of quick dip confinement.[153]

The court should use a modification order, Form AOC-CR-609, to impose a quick dip.

Probation officers may impose a similar form of quick dip confinement through delegated authority.[154] If an officer determines that the probationer has violated a condition imposed by the court, he or she may seek a supervisor's approval to impose a quick dip. Prior to imposing it, the officer must present the probationer with a violation report and advise him or her of the rights (1) to a court hearing on the violation, (2) to a lawyer, (3) to request witnesses who have relevant information concerning the alleged violation, and (4) to examine any witnesses or evidence. If the probationer executes a waiver of those rights—signed by the probationer and two probation officers

REVOCATION

CONFINEMENT IN RESPONSE TO VIOLATION (CRV)

QUICK DIP

SPECIAL PROBATION (SPLIT)

CONTEMPT

EXTENSION

MODIFICATION

TRANSFER TO UNSUPERVISED PROBATION

TERMINATION

CONTINUATION WITHOUT MODIFICATION

---

150. G.S. 15A-1344(e) ("No confinement other than an activated suspended sentence may be required beyond the period of probation . . . .").

151. G.S. 15A-1343(a1)(3).

152. G.S. 15A-1344(d).

153. G.S. 7A-313. This $40 per day jail fee is not to be confused with the $10 per day jail fee for pretrial confinement. The $10 fee is a cost that may be waived only with findings for just cause, as provided in G.S. 7A-304(a). The $40 fee is discretionary, and a judge may choose not to impose it without any special findings.

154. *See infra* notes 212–221 and accompanying text.

acting as witnesses—the officer may impose the quick dip.[155] No jail fees apply to quick dips imposed by a probation officer.

It is unclear whether judges and probation officers draw from the same statutory allotment of quick dip days per month, but Community Corrections assumes as a matter of policy that they do. A probation officer may exercise delegated authority to impose a quick dip only when the officer determines that the probationer has failed to comply with one or more conditions of probation imposed by the court and the probationer has waived his or her rights to a hearing and counsel on the alleged violation.[156] By statute, a probation officer may impose a quick dip for any violation in a Structured Sentencing case, but not in any DWI case.

1. Revocation after Two Quick Dips

Structured Sentencing misdemeanants placed on probation on or after December 1, 2015—the same cohort of probationers for whom CRV was repealed, as described above—are eligible for revocation in response to any violation after they have received two periods of quick dip confinement in response to prior technical violations, imposed either by a judge as a modification of probation or by a probation officer through delegated authority.[157] In that way, quick dips have replaced CRV as the sanction that serves as a first and second "strike" for technical violations, paving the way for a probationer to later be revoked for a subsequent technical violation.

Not all quick dips qualify as "strikes," however. The quick dips must have been imposed in response to a technical violation (not a new crime or absconding), and the second period of confinement must have been imposed for a violation that occurred after the defendant served the first quick dip.[158] By policy, when a probation officer imposes a quick dip, he or she must file a record of it with the clerk of court. Probation violation reports filed with the court for subsequent violations will indicate how many quick dips the probationer has already served, if any, which gives some indication as to the person's eligibility for revocation for a technical violation. However, the record of quick dips on the violation report does not indicate whether the quick dip was imposed in response to a technical violation, or whether the second period of confinement was imposed for a violation that occurred after the defendant served the first period of confinement. Therefore, a more careful examination of the record may be required in some cases to determine the probationer's status.

If a person who previously served quick dips later has his or her probation revoked, any time spent imprisoned for the quick dips must be credited to the defendant's activated sentence.[159]

---

155. G.S. 15A-1343.2.

156. *Id.*

157. G.S. 15A-1344(d2).

158. *Id.*

159. *Id.*; G.S. 15-196.1.

D. Special Probation (Split Sentence)

With any finding of violation, the court may modify probation to place the defendant on special probation—often referred to as a split sentence. Special probation confinement may be as little as one day, but no more than one-fourth the maximum sentence imposed (or, in the case of impaired driving, one-fourth the maximum penalty allowed by law). The judge may order the confinement to be served in a local jail or in prison, and in continuous or noncontinuous periods. Noncontinuous periods (like weekends, for example) must be served in a local jail.[160] When a defendant serves a split sentence in the jail, the judge may, in his or her discretion, impose a $40 per day jail fee on the defendant.[161]

For split sentences added as a modification of probation, no confinement other than an activated sentence may be required beyond the period of probation or two years from the time the special probation is imposed, whichever comes first.[162] In other words, the split confinement must end when probation expires.

Special probation is more flexible than CRV in terms of length, manner of service, and place of confinement, and so it may be a useful response option in some cases. It does not, however, count as a technical violation "strike" that puts the defendant on a path to eligibility for revocation for subsequent technical violations.

E. Contempt

If a probationer willfully violates a condition of probation, the court may hold him or her in criminal contempt in lieu of revocation.[163] The probation statute dealing with contempt incorporates by reference the procedures set out in Article 1 of G.S. Chapter 5A. As a result, before a probationer may be punished with contempt, he or she should receive notice as provided in G.S. 5A-15(a) (probation officers use a special violation report, Form DCC-10C, in cases where they will recommend contempt), and violations punished through contempt must be proved beyond a reasonable doubt under G.S. 5A-15(f). Punishment for criminal contempt may not exceed 30 days. Time

REVOCATION

CONFINEMENT IN RESPONSE TO VIOLATION (CRV)

QUICK DIP

SPECIAL PROBATION (SPLIT)

CONTEMPT

EXTENSION

MODIFICATION

TRANSFER TO UNSUPERVISED PROBATION

TERMINATION

CONTINUATION WITHOUT MODIFICATION

---

160. G.S. 15A-1344(e). When determining the maximum term of special probation confinement permissible in response to a probation violation, the court should take into account any special probation confinement ordered at sentencing under G.S. 15A-1351(a). The total of all special probation confinement ordered under both statutes should not exceed one-fourth the maximum sentence. State v. Younts, 794 S.E.2d 923 (2016) (unpublished).

161. G.S. 7A-313. This $40 per day jail fee is not to be confused with the $10 per day jail fee for pretrial confinement. The $10 fee is a cost that may be waived only with findings for just cause, as provided in G.S. 7A-304(a). The $40 fee is discretionary, and a judge may choose not to impose it without any requirement for special findings.

162. G.S. 15A-1344(e).

163. G.S. 15A-1344(e1).

spent imprisoned for contempt in response to a probation violation counts for credit against the suspended sentence if that sentence is eventually activated.[164]

Contempt does not count as a technical violation "strike" that puts the defendant on a path to eligibility for revocation for subsequent technical violations.

F. Extension

The General Statutes describe two different types of probation extensions: *ordinary extensions* under G.S. 15A-1344(d) and *special-purpose extensions* under G.S. 15A-1343.2. (The terms "ordinary" and "special-purpose" are used here for clarity; they do not appear in the General Statutes.)

1. Ordinary Extensions

Ordinary extensions may, after notice and hearing, be ordered at *any time* prior to the expiration of probation for "good cause shown" (no violation need have occurred).[165] The total maximum probation period, including any ordinary extensions, is 5 years, except in deferred prosecution and conditional discharge cases, in which it is 2 years.[166] A defendant's probation period may be extended multiple times under G.S. 15A-1344(d), provided the total probation period does not exceed 5 years. For instance, a defendant initially placed on probation for 12 months could, under G.S. 15A-1344(d), have that probation extended to 24 months at one hearing, then to 60 months at a later hearing.

For many years, probation officers would routinely coordinate ordinary extensions outside of open court, getting the prosecutor, the defendant, and then the judge to sign a modification order in chambers or elsewhere for a defendant who consented to the extension. However, unpublished appellate decisions have called attention to the fact that no statute clearly authorizes a defendant to waive his or her right to notice and a hearing before an ordinary extension, and that the defendant is entitled to counsel before any hearing at which probation is extended.[167] With those cases in mind, Community Corrections now directs officers to seek ordinary extensions only in a courtroom hearing, after having given notice of the hearing to the probationer.[168]

---

164. State v. Belcher, 173 N.C. App. 620 (2005). *See also* Jamie Markham, *Jail Credit for Probation Contempt*, UNC Sch. of Gov't: N.C. Crim. L. Blog (Dec. 13, 2012), nccriminallaw.sog.unc.edu/jail-credit-for-probation-contempt.

165. GS 15A-1344(d).

166. GS 15A-1342(a).

167. *See* State v. Craig, 798 S.E.2d 438 (2017) (unpublished); State v. Lawrence, 197 N.C. App. 630 (2009) (unpublished). *See also* Jamie Markham, *In-Chambers Modifications and Extensions of Probation*, UNC Sch. of Gov't: N.C. Crim. L. Blog (Nov. 17, 2016), nccriminallaw.sog.unc.edu/chambers-modifications-extensions-probation.

168. *See* Jamie Markham, *A Change to Probation's Policy on Ordinary Extensions*, UNC Sch. of Gov't: N.C. Crim. L. Blog (Aug. 8, 2017), nccriminallaw.sog.unc.edu/change-probations-policy-ordinary-extensions/.

2. Special-Purpose Extensions

Special-purpose extensions can be used to extend the probationer's period of probation by up to 3 years beyond the original period of probation if all of the following criteria are met:

1. The probationer consents to the extension.
2. The extension is being ordered during the last 6 months of the *original* period of probation.[169]
3. The extension is necessary to complete a program of *restitution* or to complete *medical or psychiatric treatment*.[170]

Completion of substance abuse treatment is not "medical or psychiatric treatment," and thus not a valid reason for a special purpose extension.[171]

Extensions for these special purposes are generally understood to allow the court to extend a period of probation beyond 5 years, which makes the maximum possible probation period in a single case 8 years. However, only when the *original* period is 5 years can probation be extended to as long as 8 years under this provision, because a special-purpose extension must take place within the last 6 months of the *original* period of probation. If probation has previously been extended, the offender is no longer in his or her *original* period of probation, and is thus ineligible for further extension under G.S. 15A-1343.2 or 15A-1342(a). Thus, a special-purpose extension generally may happen only once in the life of a particular probation case.

A special-purpose extension probably is permissible in a conditional discharge or deferred prosecution case.[172] If so, then probation in those cases—typically capped at 2 years—could be extended to as long 5 years when the original period of probation was 2 years and the three eligibility criteria listed above apply.

G. Modification

After notice and hearing and for good cause shown, the court may modify probation at any time prior to its expiration or termination.[173] There need not be a finding of violation to empower the court to modify probation; modifications may be made without violation for good cause. With or without a violation, a defendant generally

---

169. *See* State v. Gorman, 221 N.C. App. 330, 727 S.E.2d 731 (2012) (vacating an extension order entered in the third year of a 60-month period of probation because it was ordered too early).

170. G.S. 15A-1343.2; -1342(a).

171. State v. Peed, ___ N.C. App. ___, 810 S.E.2d 777 (2018) ("We conclude that the General Assembly did not intend for a probation condition to complete 'substance abuse treatment' to be synonymous with (or a subset of) a probation condition to complete 'medical or psychiatric treatment.'").

172. One version of the special-purpose extension law appears in G.S. 15A-1342(a)— the same subsection that sets the 2-year maximum probation period for conditional discharge and deferred prosecution cases, making it hard to argue that the provision does not also apply in those cases.

173. G.S. 15A-1344(d).

REVOCATION

CONFINEMENT IN RESPONSE TO VIOLATION (CRV)

QUICK DIP

SPECIAL PROBATION (SPLIT)

CONTEMPT

EXTENSION

MODIFICATION

TRANSFER TO UNSUPERVISED PROBATION

TERMINATION

CONTINUATION WITHOUT MODIFICATION

has a right to be present at any hearing at which probation is modified, even if the modification is minor[174]—although the hearing may be held in the absence of a defendant who fails to appear after a reasonable effort to notify him or her.[175]

Upon a finding that an offender sentenced to community punishment has violated one or more conditions of probation, the court may add conditions of probation that would otherwise make the sentence an intermediate punishment.[176]

If any conditions are modified, the probationer must receive a written statement of the modification.[177] Probation may not later be revoked for violation of a new or modified condition unless the defendant had written notice that the condition applied to him or her; oral notice alone is insufficient.[178]

H. Transfer to Unsupervised Probation

A judge may transfer a supervised probationer to unsupervised probation at any time. The court may also authorize a probation officer to transfer a defendant to unsupervised probation after all money owed by the defendant is paid to the clerk. Additionally, a probation officer has independent authority to transfer a low-risk misdemeanant from supervised to unsupervised probation if the misdemeanant is not subject to any special conditions and was placed on probation solely for the collection of court-ordered payments.[179]

A separate statutory provision in Chapter 20 governs transfers to unsupervised probation for impaired drivers subject to Level Three, Four, or Five punishment. If the defendant is initially placed on supervised probation in those cases, the court must authorize the probation officer to place the defendant on unsupervised probation when he or she has completed community service; paid all fines, court costs, and fees; or both.[180]

A probationer subject to the special conditions of probation applicable to sex offenders may not be placed on unsupervised probation.[181]

---

174. *See* State v. Willis, 199 N.C. App. 309 (2009) (vacating a condition that was modified outside the defendant's presence to prohibit him from having more than one animal "in his possession" to prohibiting him from having more than one animal "in his possession *or on his premises*" (emphasis added)).

175. G.S. 15A-1344(d).

176. G.S. 15A-1344(a).

177. G.S. 15A-1343(c).

178. State v. Seek, 152 N.C. App. 237 (2002); State v. Suggs, 92 N.C. App. 112 (1988).

179. G.S. 15A-1343(g).

180. G.S. 20-179(r). *See generally* Shea Riggsbee Denning, The Law of Impaired Driving and Related Implied Consent Offenses in North Carolina (UNC School of Government, 2014), 182.

181. G.S. 15A-1343(b2).

I. Termination

The court may terminate probation at any time if warranted by the conduct of the defendant and "the ends of justice."[182] Although frequently used in practice, the concept of "unsuccessful" or "unsatisfactory" termination does not appear in the General Statutes or appellate case law and carries no defined legal significance.

When a probationer has a probation period greater than 3 years, the probation officer must bring him or her back before the court after 3 years of probation so that the court can review the case to determine whether to terminate probation.[183] Though the statute styles the review as mandatory, a failure to complete it does not deprive the court of later jurisdiction over the case.[184]

Termination of a probation case does not, on its own, extinguish monetary obligations (costs, fines, and other fees) the defendant might owe in relation to the case. If the court wishes to remit or otherwise forgive those obligations, it should affirmatively do so—perhaps especially in Chapter 20 cases, where an unpaid obligation could trigger a driver's license revocation.[185]

REVOCATION

CONFINEMENT IN RESPONSE TO VIOLATION (CRV)

QUICK DIP

SPECIAL PROBATION (SPLIT)

CONTEMPT

EXTENSION

MODIFICATION

TRANSFER TO UNSUPERVISED PROBATION

TERMINATION

CONTINUATION WITHOUT MODIFICATION

J. Continuation without Modification

Whether or not the court finds a violation at a hearing, it may always continue the defendant on probation under the same conditions. This is sometimes referred to as reinstating the defendant's probation.

K. Electing to Serve a Sentence

Some probationers ask to "invoke" their sentence—that is, to have their probation revoked so they may serve their remaining suspended sentence. There is no clear legal authority to do that. Prior law allowing a defendant to elect to serve a sentence was repealed in 1995, effective for offenses occurring on or after January 1, 1997.[186] A defendant may admit to a violation of probation, but for violations occurring on or after December 1, 2011, the admitted-to violation must be a new criminal offense or absconding to allow the court to revoke. For defendants with short suspended sentences, an admission to a technical violation might allow for a CRV period long enough to use up the defendant's entire remaining suspended sentence, which is functionally similar to a revocation.

Defendants on probation for felony offenses committed on or after December 1, 2011, should note that they will be released to post-release supervision upon their

---

182. G.S. 15A-1342(b).
183. G.S. 15A-1342(d).
184. State v. Benfield, 22 N.C. App. 330 (1974).
185. G.S. 20-24.1.
186. G.S. 15A-1341(c), *repealed by* S.L. 1995-429.

release from imprisonment and that, by statute, PRS cannot be refused.[187] Thus, the incentive to elect to serve active time may be diminished.[188]

V. Violation Hearings in Diversion Cases

A. Deferred Prosecutions

When a person on probation pursuant to a deferred prosecution agreement under G.S. 15A-1341(a1) is alleged to have violated probation, the violation must be reported to the court and to the district attorney in the district in which the agreement was entered.[189] The court, not the district attorney, determines through ordinary probation hearing procedures whether a violation occurred and whether to "order that charges as to which prosecution has been deferred be brought to trial."[190] The North Carolina Attorney General's office has advised that probation matters in deferred prosecution cases should be managed only by the court of the district in which the agreement was entered into, as "[b]ringing the charges to trial would be the responsibility of only the district attorney who brought the charges."[191] Under G.S. 143B-708(e), violation hearings initiated by community service staff may be held in the county in which a deferred prosecution agreement was imposed, the county in which the alleged violation occurred, or the offender's county of residence. In light of the guidance from the Attorney General's office, however, the best practice is probably to hold the hearing where the agreement was imposed, notwithstanding the statute's broader authorization.

B. Conditional Discharge

A conditional discharge is a diversionary option through which a convicted defendant may be placed on probation without entry of judgment. If the defendant succeeds on probation, the court discharges the defendant and dismisses the proceeding without adjudication of guilt. If the defendant violates probation, the court may enter an adjudication of guilt and sentence the defendant. Various statutes give a trial judge authority to impose a conditional discharge in certain circumstances, including G.S. 15A-1341(a4) (misdemeanors and low-level felonies committed by certain defendants), G.S. 15A-1341(a3) (prostitution), and G.S. 90-96 (certain drug crimes).

---

187. G.S. 15A-1368.2(b).

188. For a lengthier discussion of the issues that arise when a probationer attempts to invoke his or her sentence, see MARKHAM, THE NORTH CAROLINA JUSTICE REINVESTMENT ACT, *supra* note 5, at 77–79.

189. G.S. 15A-1342(a1).

190. G.S. 15A-1344(d).

191. Advisory Letter from Elizabeth F. Parsons, N.C. Assistant Attorney Gen., to LaVee Hamer, Gen. Counsel, N.C. Dep't of Corr. (Nov. 1, 2010).

In general, violation hearings for conditional discharge cases should be treated under the same rules applicable to ordinary probation cases. Violations must be timely filed and heard in the same manner as violations in ordinary post-conviction cases.[192] As in deferred prosecution cases, the district of conviction is probably the best venue for a probation hearing in a conditional discharge case; the defendant must be sentenced if revoked, and there is no clear authority for any court outside of the district of conviction to conduct the sentencing.

When a conditional discharge probationer is found in violation of a term or condition of probation, the court may revoke the probation, enter an adjudication of guilt, and proceed as otherwise provided.[193] Revocation is not required in the event of a violation but is, rather, within the trial court's discretion.

C. Response Options in Diversion Cases

The law is not crystal clear about a judge's authority to respond to violations of probation in deferred prosecution and conditional discharge cases. For both types of cases, the relevant statutes typically say that probation is "as provided in this Article,"[194] referring to Article 82—the statutory article governing ordinary probation. That language could be read to allow the court to take any action in a diversion case that it may take in an ordinary probation case. However, some portions of the ordinary probation framework are not a good fit in diversion cases. For example, any response that includes confinement (CRV, quick dips, and special probation) is probably off limits for diversion defendants who have not yet been sentenced, as they do not yet have a suspended sentence from which to draw creditable confinement days. Even contempt is problematic in that regard, as contempt ordered in response to a probation violation counts for credit against a defendant's suspended sentence.[195]

It is likewise unclear whether the typical limits on a judge's authority to revoke probation (revocation only for a new criminal offense or absconding) apply in diversion cases. On the one hand, in *State v. Burns* the court of appeals held that ordinary probation rules apply in conditional discharge cases in the absence of a provision to the contrary.[196] That rule lends support to the argument that "revocation" of diversion cases should, like ordinary cases, be limited to new criminal offense violations and absconding. (The third pathway to revocation, for probationers with two prior technical violations, would not apply to diversion cases—assuming they are indeed exempt from confinement-based sanctions, as described above.) On the other hand, the statutes governing noncompliance with conditional discharge probation do not generally use the words "revoke" or "revocation" at all. Instead, they refer to entering

---

192. State v. Burns, 171 N.C. App. 759, 761 (2005) ("In the absence of a provision to the contrary, and except where specifically excluded, the general probation provisions found in Article 82 of [G.S.] Chapter 15A apply to probation imposed under [G.S.] 90-96.").
193. G.S. 15A-1341(a6); 90-96(a).
194. *E.g.,* G.S. 15A-1341(a4).
195. *See* State v. Belcher, 173 N.C. App. 620 (2005).
196. *Burns*, 171 N.C. App. 759.

judgment and proceeding as otherwise provided (for conditional discharges) and ordering charges brought to trial (for deferred prosecutions), perhaps indicating that the conclusion of these cases is something altogether different from an ordinary probation revocation, and thus not subject to the same background rules. For the time being, it appears to be an open question.

One exception to this ambiguity applies to defendants subject to conditional discharge under G.S. 90-96(a1) (the less frequently used conditional discharge found in G.S. 90-96—most defendants will fall under subsection (a)). Subsection (a1) specifically provides that a person's "failure to complete successfully an approved program of instruction at a drug education school" constitutes grounds to revoke. The subsection defines this failure broadly to include failing to attend classes without an excuse, failing to complete the course in a timely fashion, or failing to pay the required fee. If the court receives an instructor's report about a person's failure to complete the drug education school, it must revoke probation.

If probation for a deferred prosecution or conditional discharge expires or the court terminates it early, the defendant is immune from prosecution of the charges deferred or discharged and dismissed.[197] In conditional discharge cases, it is unclear whether that immunity from prosecution requires the court to presume that the defendant has fulfilled the terms and conditions of the conditional discharge probation in a way that obliges the court to dismiss the conviction and discharge the defendant. To avoid that uncertainty, any scheduled review of a defendant's progress in a conditional discharge case should take place long enough before the case expires to allow the court sufficient time to respond to any alleged noncompliance.[198]

VI. Violations in Interstate Compact Cases

Some probationers are supervised in North Carolina on behalf of another state under the Interstate Compact for Adult Offender Supervision (the Compact).[199] These probationers are subject to the conditions of supervision imposed by the sending state, plus any conditions North Carolina has imposed under the Compact rules.[200] In those cases, when the probationer has allegedly violated a condition of probation, he or she may be arrested and detained for up to 15 days pending a preliminary hearing. Probation officers must coordinate the arrest through North Carolina's Interstate Compact Administrator in Raleigh, which issues an *Authority to Detain and Hold* form

---

197. G.S. 15A-1342(j).

198. *See* Jamie Markham, *G.S. 90-96 Limbo*, UNC Sch. of Gov't: N.C. Crim. L. Blog (Feb. 4, 2014), nccriminallaw.sog.unc.edu/g-s-90-96-limbo.

199. *See* G.S. 148-65.4 through -65.8.

200. Interstate Compact for Adult Offender Supervision, Rule 4.103 (allowing the receiving state to "impose a condition on an offender if that condition would have been imposed on an offender sentenced in the receiving state"), https://www.interstatecompact.org/sites/default/files/pdf/legal/ICAOS-2018-Rules-ENG_0.pdf.

(roughly equivalent to an order for arrest) accompanied by an arrest warrant from the sending state. Probationers arrested under the Compact are not entitled to bail.[201]

Unless the defendant waives it, the preliminary hearing is typically conducted in the local jail by a hearing officer employed by the Division of Adult Correction and Juvenile Justice, although a North Carolina judge is also empowered to hold the hearing. Prior to the hearing, the defendant must be permitted to consult with anyone whose assistance he or she reasonably desires. At the hearing, the defendant has the right to confront and examine anyone who has made allegations against him or her, unless the hearing officer determines that such confrontation would present a danger of harm to the accuser. The defendant can present proof, including affidavits and other evidence, supporting his or her contentions.[202] It is unclear whether North Carolina's blanket statutory entitlement to appointed counsel for probation violations applies to preliminary hearings for indigent Compact probationers. Regardless, some indigent defendants will be entitled to appointed counsel as a constitutional matter— those who make a colorable claim that they did not commit the alleged violation, those with substantial and complex reasons that justify or mitigate the violation, or those who might be incapable of speaking effectively for themselves.[203]

If the hearing officer finds probable cause to believe that a violation occurred, the sending state may retake the defendant for a final violation hearing in that state. The defendant remains in custody in North Carolina as may be necessary to arrange for the retaking.[204]

In cases where another state is supervising a probationer on North Carolina's behalf, the preliminary hearing is held in the receiving state (unless the probationer waives it). If probable cause exists, the defendant is subject to being returned to North Carolina for a final violation hearing held under the ordinary procedures described elsewhere in this book.[205]

---

201. G.S. 148-65.8(a). The fact that the arrest warrant will originate from the sending state—which retains ultimate jurisdiction over the case—can sometimes lead Compact probationers to be misidentified as fugitives subject to the extradition process.

202. G.S. 148-65.8(c).

203. Gagnon v. Scarpelli, 411 U.S. 778, 790–91 (1973).

204. G.S. 148-65.8(c1).

205. G.S. 148-65.8(d).

VII. Other Issues That May Arise at a Violation Hearing

A. Credit for Time Served

If probation is revoked and a sentence is activated, the probationer must get credit for the following time under G.S. 15-196.1:

- pretrial confinement,[206]
- the active portion of a split sentence,[207]
- time spent at DART Cherry (the state-run residential treatment facility for chemically dependent males) as a condition of probation,[208]
- pre-sentence commitment for study,[209]
- hospitalization to determine competency to stand trial,[210]
- time spent in confinement in another state awaiting extradition when the defendant was held in the other state based solely on North Carolina charges,[211]
- time spent in the now-defunct IMPACT boot camp program,[212]
- time spent imprisoned for contempt under G.S. 15A-1344(e1),[213]
- "quick dip" confinement time imposed by a probation officer or judge,[214] and
- time imprisoned as confinement in response to violation (CRV).[215] However, when a person on probation for multiple felony offenses serves concurrent CRVs for sentences that wind up running consecutively upon revocation, credit is applied to only one of the defendant's consecutive activated sentences.[216]

Credit should not be awarded for the following:

- Time spent under electronic house arrest.[217]
- Time spent at a privately run residential treatment program as a condition of probation (in a non-DWI case).[218]

---

206. G.S. 15-196.1.
207. State v. Farris, 336 N.C. 553 (1994).
208. State v. Lutz, 177 N.C. App. 140 (2006). Time spent at Black Mountain Substance Abuse Treatment Center for Women, the equivalent to DART Cherry for women, probably also qualifies for credit under *Lutz*.
209. State v. Powell, 11 N.C. App. 194 (1971).
210. State v. Lewis, 18 N.C. App. 681 (1973).
211. Childers v. Laws, 558 F. Supp. 1284 (W.D.N.C. 1983).
212. State v. Hearst, 356 N.C. 132 (2002).
213. State v. Belcher, 173 N.C. App. 620 (2005).
214. G.S. 15A-1344(d2).
215. *Id.*
216. G.S. 15-196.2.
217. State v. Jarman, 140 N.C. App. 198 (2000).
218. State v. Stephenson, 213 N.C. App. 621 (2011).

B. Delegated Authority

For cases sentenced under Structured Sentencing, the law allows a probation officer to impose certain additional probation conditions on an offender without action by the court.[219] Delegated authority applies only to cases sentenced under Structured Sentencing;[220] it does not apply in impaired driving cases or to any case sentenced under older law.

The sentencing court may find in any case that it is not appropriate to delegate authority to a probation officer. Probationary judgment forms include a check-box for the court to withhold delegated authority. The probation modification form (AOC-CR-609) likewise includes check-boxes for the court to delegate authority that was previously withheld or to withhold authority previously delegated. If the court has withheld delegated authority, the probation officer may not impose additional conditions of supervision.

Which conditions a probation officer may add through delegated authority depends on whether the probationer was sentenced to community punishment or intermediate punishment. In community punishment cases, the officer may add the following conditions:

- Perform up to 20 hours of community service and pay the fee prescribed by law.
- Report to the offender's probation officer on a frequency to be determined by the officer.
- Submit to substance abuse assessment, monitoring, or treatment.
- Submit to house arrest with electronic monitoring.
- Submit to "quick-dip" confinement, a period or periods of confinement in a local confinement facility, for a total of no more than 6 days per month in any 3 separate months during the period of probation. This confinement may be imposed only as 2- or 3-day consecutive periods.
- Submit to an electronically monitored curfew.
- Participate in an educational or vocational skills development program, including an evidence-based program.[221]

In intermediate punishment cases, the officer may add any of the conditions permitted in community cases plus the following conditions:

- Perform up to 50 hours of community service and pay the fee prescribed by law.
- Submit to continuous alcohol monitoring when abstinence from alcohol consumption has been specified as a condition of probation.
- Submit to satellite-based monitoring (SBM) if the defendant is an offender of the type described by G.S. 14-208.40(a)(2).[222]

---

219. G.S. 15A-1343.2(e) and (f).

220. G.S. 15A-1343.2(a) ("This section applies only to persons sentenced under Article 81B of this Chapter.").

221. G.S. 15A-1343.2(e).

222. G.S. 15A-1343.2(f).

The circumstances in which officers may exercise delegated authority are identical for community cases and intermediate cases. An officer may exercise delegated authority upon a determination that the offender has failed to comply with one or more court-imposed conditions. An officer may not exercise delegated authority in response to violations of officer-imposed conditions.[223]

A probation officer may also add delegated authority conditions other than quick dips without a violation if the offender is determined to be high risk based on the results of a risk assessment. The statute does not define *high risk*, but the Division of Adult Correction and Juvenile Justice (DACJJ) has determined as a matter of policy that it means offenders with risk assessment scores of 50 or higher.[224]

When a probation officer imposes a delegated authority condition other than a quick dip, the probationer may file a motion with the court to review the new condition. The law does not describe the exact nature of the hearing on such a motion or set any timeline for how quickly it must be held. The offender must be given notice (presumably by the probation officer) of the right to seek court review of any officer-imposed conditions.[225]

Whether a specific violation to which a probation officer has responded through delegated authority may later serve as the basis for a violation found by the court is not clear. The statutes say that "nothing in [the delegated authority] section shall be construed to limit the availability of the procedures authorized under G.S. 15A-1345"[226] (the probation violation hearing statute), but this provision is susceptible to multiple interpretations. That may simply mean that a probation officer is not required in any case to exercise delegated authority but, rather, may always bring violations before the court for review in the first instance. Alternatively, the provision could be read to mean that violation proceedings before the court under G.S. 15A-1345 are available without limit, even in cases where the officer has already exercised delegated authority. Regardless, Community Corrections policy instructs probation officers that noncompliance addressed through the delegated authority process cannot be included on any future violation report.[227]

The court may later respond to violations of conditions added by a probation officer through delegated authority in the same way it may respond to violations of any other condition. Before responding, the court should verify that the condition was added through a proper exercise of the officer's delegated authority. A probation officer may

---

223. *Id.*

224. Community Corrections Policy, *supra* note 24, at § C.0606. For a discussion of the risk-needs assessment used by DACJJ's Community Corrections section, including the supervision levels into which probationers are assigned, see Jamie Markham, *Probation's Risk-Needs Assessment Process in a Nutshell*, UNC Sch. of Gov't: N.C. Crim. L. Blog (Aug. 8, 2012), nccriminallaw.sog.unc.edu/probations-risk-needs-assessment-process-in-a-nutshell.

225. G.S. 15A-1343.2(e) and (f).

226. *Id.*

227. Community Corrections Policy, *supra* note 24, at § D.0205(f) ("Once noncompliance has been addressed through the delegated authority process, it cannot be included on any future violation report.").

not respond to subsequent violations of conditions added through delegated authority with *additional* delegated authority, as the law limits violation-based delegated authority to violations of conditions imposed by the court.[228]

C. Work Release

Under G.S. 15A-1351(f), the sentencing court may recommend or, with the consent of the defendant, order work release for a misdemeanant. When a defendant is sentenced to probation, that recommendation should not be made until probation is revoked and the sentence of imprisonment is activated.[229]

D. Civil Judgments for Monetary Obligations

Certain monetary obligations may be docketed as a civil judgment against the defendant at the end of a probation case. Unpaid fines and costs may, upon default, be docketed as a lien on the defendant's real estate.[230] Attorney fees and the attorney appointment fee are civil judgments against the defendant from the point of imposition, but when they are ordered as a condition of probation, they are not docketed and indexed until the date probation expires, is terminated, or is revoked.[231]

Restitution in cases covered under the Crime Victims' Rights Act (CVRA) may be docketed as a civil judgment if the restitution amount exceeds $250. In cases where such restitution is ordered as a condition of probation, the judgment may not be executed upon the defendant's property until the clerk is notified that the defendant's probation has been terminated or revoked and the judge has made a finding that restitution in a sum certain remains owed.[232] The finding that a restitution balance is due upon revocation or termination of probation should be made on Form AOC-CR-612.

E. License Forfeiture upon Revocation

If a felony probationer either "refuses probation" or has probation revoked for failing, in the revoking court's estimation, "to make reasonable efforts to comply with the conditions of probation," the probationer automatically forfeits all licensing privileges.[233] The court may use side two of Form AOC-CR-317 to order the forfeiture, which covers driver's licenses (regular and commercial), occupational licenses, and hunting and fishing licenses.

---

228. G.S. 15A-1343.2.
229. G.S. 148-33.1(i).
230. G.S. 15A-1365.
231. G.S. 7A-455(c).
232. G.S. 15A-1340.38.
233. G.S. 15A-1331.1 (formerly G.S. 15A-1331A, *recodified by* S.L. 2012-194, § 45.(a)).

The forfeiture lasts "for the full term of the period the individual is placed on probation by the sentencing court at the time of conviction for the offense."[234] The forfeiture period must end when the probationer's original term of probation would have expired. For instance, a person whose probation is revoked 23 months into a 24-month period of probation can face only a 1-month license forfeiture under G.S. 15A-1331.1 (not a 24-month forfeiture period beginning at the time of revocation).[235] For purposes of filling out the AOC-CR-317, the beginning date of the forfeiture typically will be the date of the revocation hearing, and the end date will be the date the original period of probation ordered by the sentencing court would have expired.

F. Driver's License Forfeiture for Violations Related to Community Service

If a court determines that a defendant has willfully failed to comply with a requirement to complete community service, the court shall revoke any driver's license issued to the person until the community service requirement has been met.[236]

G. Finding of Violation as a Potential Aggravating Factor

If the court finds the defendant to be in willful violation of a condition of his or her supervision, that finding may serve as an aggravating factor in the sentencing of any crime committed during the 10 years following the finding.[237] Only findings of violation by the "court" (or, in the case of post-release supervision, by the Post-Release Supervision and Parole Commission) qualify the defendant for the aggravating factor. A violation found by a probation officer through delegated authority cannot support the aggravating factor.

VIII. Selected Defenses to Probation Violations

A. Improper Period of Probation

G.S. 15A-1343.2(d) sets out the presumptive lengths for periods of probation imposed under Structured Sentencing as follows:

- Misdemeanants sentenced to community punishment: 6–18 months,
- Misdemeanants sentenced to intermediate punishment: 12–24 months,

---

234. G.S. 15A-1331.1(b).
235. State v. Kerrin, 209 N.C. App. 72 (2011).
236. G.S. 143B-708(e).
237. G.S. 15A-1340.16(d)(12a).

- Felons sentenced to community punishment: 12–30 months, and
- Felons sentenced to intermediate punishment: 18–36 months.

The sentencing court may always deviate from these defaults and order probation of up to 5 years if it "finds at the time of sentencing that a longer period of probation is necessary."[238] The required finding is merely that a longer period of probation is necessary; the statute does not require the court to offer a detailed rationale.[239] There is a check-box on the suspended sentence judgment forms to indicate that the judge has made the requisite finding.

Sometimes a court sentences a defendant to a probation term longer than the defaults set out above without making the requisite findings. When the error is discovered early on and the defendant appeals, the appellate courts remand the case for resentencing with instructions to the trial court to make the requisite finding or order a shorter period of probation.[240] If the error is not discovered until the defendant has already violated probation, the probationer could file a motion for appropriate relief under G.S. 15A-1415(b)(8) on the ground that the sentence was unauthorized at the time imposed. If the case would have expired if the probation term had been within the durational limits set out in the statute, the defendant will have an argument that the court lacks jurisdiction over the violation, especially if the violation occurred after a lawful period would have ended.

Along similar lines, if an earlier extension of probation was improper and the period of probation would have expired but for the improper extension, the court loses authority to act on the case.[241]

B. Willfulness

Probation may not be revoked unless a violation was willful or without a lawful excuse.[242] The rule has also been stated that a defendant's probation should not be revoked because of circumstances beyond his or her control.[243] For instance, a sex offender probationer's failure to find an approved residence was not a willful violation when he was arrested by his probation officer before having a meaningful opportunity to find a place to live upon his release from prison.[244] On the other hand, a defendant's

---

238. G.S. 15A-1343.2(d).

239. State v. Wilkerson, 223 N.C. App. 195 (2002) (holding that the trial court "went beyond the statutory requirement" by recording factual support for its decision that a 60-month period of probation was necessary).

240. *See, e.g.,* State v. Riley, 202 N.C. App. 299 (2010).

241. State v. Gorman, 221 N.C. App. 330 (2012); State v. Satanek, 190 N.C. App. 653 (2008); State v. Reinhardt, 183 N.C. App. 291 (2007).

242. State v. Hewett, 270 N.C. 348 (1967).

243. State v. Duncan, 270 N.C. 241 (1967).

244. State v. Talbert, 221 N.C. App. 650 (2012); State v. Askew, 221 N.C. App. 659 (2012) (similar facts).

explanation that she was addicted to drugs was not a lawful excuse for violating probation by failing to complete a drug education program.[245]

Procedurally, once the state establishes that a defendant failed to comply with a condition of probation, the burden is on the defendant to produce evidence that the failure to comply was not willful. If the defendant does not offer evidence of his or her inability to comply, the State's evidence of the failure to comply is sufficient to justify revocation of probation.[246] If a defendant presents evidence of his or her inability to comply, the court must consider that evidence and make findings of fact clearly showing that it considered the evidence.[247] For example, in *State v. Floyd*,[248] the trial court erred by failing to make findings of fact that clearly showed it considered the defendant's evidence that he was unable to pay the cost of his sexual abuse treatment program. The defendant presented evidence, corroborated by his probation officer, that he was unable to pay for the program because he had lost his job and that he would have completed the program if he could have afforded it.

When the alleged violation is the nonpayment of a fine or costs, the court must consider the "issues and procedures" specified in G.S. 15A-1364 at the violation hearing.[249] That statute says the defendant must be given an opportunity to show that he or she was unable to pay. The burden is on the probationer to show that he or she could not pay despite an effort made in good faith to do so.[250] If the defendant meets that burden, the court may (1) allow additional time for the defendant to pay, (2) reduce the amount owed, or (3) remit the obligation altogether.[251] As a constitutional matter, a person cannot be incarcerated for failing to pay money if he or she has made a bona fide effort to pay, unless alternative measures are inadequate to meet society's interest in punishment and deterrence.[252]

C. Invalid Condition of Probation

The court may not revoke probation for a violation of an invalid condition of supervision. By statute, the regular conditions of probation imposed pursuant to G.S. 15A-1343(b) are in every case valid.[253] Similarly, the statutory special conditions set out in G.S. 15A-1343(b1) are presumptively valid in any case in which they are

---

245. State v. Stephenson, 213 N.C. App. 621 (2011). *See also* State v. Tozzi, 84 N.C. App. 517 (1987) (holding that defendant's explanation that he missed required meetings with his probation officer because he was job hunting was not a lawful excuse).

246. State v. Jones, 78 N.C. App. 507 (1985).

247. State v. Hill, 132 N.C. App. 209 (1999).

248. 213 N.C. App. 611 (2011).

249. G.S. 15A-1345(e).

250. *Jones*, 78 N.C. App. 507.

251. G.S. 15A-1345(e); -1364(c).

252. Bearden v. Georgia, 461 U.S. 660 (1983).

253. G.S. 15A-1343; -1342(g).

imposed.[254] If the court adds ad hoc special conditions of probation under authority of G.S. 15A-1343(b1)(10), those conditions must be reasonably related to the offender's rehabilitation. Any ad hoc conditions must also bear a relationship to the defendant's crime, although case law suggests that the nexus between the condition and the crime need not be particularly close.[255] The appellate courts have interpreted the catch-all provision broadly, giving trial judges "substantial discretion" in tailoring a judgment to fit a particular offender and offense.[256]

A probation condition is also considered invalid if the defendant does not receive written notice of it under G.S. 15A-1343(c). Probation may not be revoked for a violation of a condition unless the defendant had written notice that the condition applied to him or her.[257] Oral notice is not a satisfactory substitute for the written statement.[258] There is an exception to the written notice rule for the requirement to report to Community Corrections for initial processing. A verbal order to report to probation officials after sentencing is enforceable even before it is received in writing—largely as a concession to the practical reality that a defendant will not actually receive a written copy of the judgment until he or she begins the probation intake process.[259]

Probation conditions cannot place unconstitutional constraints on a probationer (such as "Go to church every Sunday" or "Get married"). For example, in *State v. Lambert*,[260] the court of appeals struck a special probation condition prohibiting a defendant from filing court documents unless they were signed and filed by a licensed attorney, as it unreasonably infringed on the defendant's fundamental right of access to the courts and his right to conduct his defense pro se. On the other hand, some limitations that would be unconstitutional for ordinary citizens are permissible as applied to probationers. For instance, a probation condition prohibiting a sex offender probationer from residing with his own minor child did not impermissibly infringe on his fundamental liberty interest as a parent to the custody and care of his child.[261]

Under G.S. 15A-1342(g), a defendant's failure to object to a condition of probation imposed under G.S. 15A-1343(b1) at the time the condition is imposed does not constitute a waiver of the right to object at a later time. The "at a later time" language of the statute does not, however, grant a perpetual right to challenge a condition of

---

254. State v. Lambert, 146 N.C. App. 360, 367 (2001) ("[W]hen the trial judge imposes one of the special conditions of probation enumerated by N.C. Gen. Stat. § 15A-1343(b1), the condition need not be reasonably related to defendant's rehabilitation because the Legislature has deemed all those special conditions appropriate to the rehabilitation of criminals and their assimilation into law-abiding society.").

255. *See, e.g.*, State v. Cooper, 304 N.C. 180 (1981) (upholding a special condition prohibiting a defendant, convicted of possession of stolen credit cards, from operating a vehicle between midnight and 5:30 a.m.).

256. State v. Harrington, 78 N.C. App. 39 (1985).

257. State v. Seek, 152 N.C. App. 237 (2002); State v. Suggs, 92 N.C. App. 112 (1988).

258. *Lambert*, 146 N.C. App. 360.

259. State v. Brown, 222 N.C. App. 738 (2012).

260. *Lambert*, 146 N.C. App. at 364.

261. State v. Strickland, 169 N.C. App. 193 (2005).

probation. Rather, the defendant must object no later than the revocation hearing.[262] Any later challenge is likely to be viewed as an impermissible collateral attack.[263]

Older cases describe a contract theory of probation, in which a probationer lacks the right to object to the appropriateness of the conditions of supervision because he or she consented to them at the outset.[264] That contract theory of probation may have been appropriate in North Carolina when defendants had a right to refuse probation under G.S. 15A-1343(c). But with the repeal of that subsection in 1995,[265] a defendant should not be considered to have consented to the conditions of supervision, and the right to challenge a condition should not be considered waived.

D. Insufficient Evidence of a Violation

A defendant may of course argue that he or she did not commit the alleged offending behavior, or that the alleged offending behavior, even if committed, did not actually violate the language of the condition at issue. For example, a probationer successfully argued in *State v. Sherrod*[266] that having bullets alone did not violate the condition restricting possession of firearms, explosive devices, or other deadly weapons. In another case, the court of appeals held that a minor child's temporary visit to a sex offender probationer's residence did not violate the condition prohibiting the probationer from residing with a minor.[267] In a case where the alleged violations were a failure to complete community service and a failure to pay monetary obligations, and in which the trial judge had left the scheduling for the community service and the repayment of the money to be determined in the discretion of the probation officer, the court of appeals held that there was insufficient evidence of a violation when the State offered no information about the payment plan and community service schedule established by the probation officer.[268]

In cases involving absconding, the appellate courts appear to undertake a more searching review of the evidence considered by the trial court judge. In *State v. Krider*, for example, the court of appeals and supreme court deemed it an abuse of discretion by the trial judge to conclude to his reasonable satisfaction that the defendant absconded based on evidence from an unidentified person that the defendant no longer lived at his designated residence.[269]

---

262. State v. Cooper, 304 N.C. 180 (1981).

263. *See infra* notes 281–283 and accompanying text.

264. *See, e.g.*, State v. Mitchell, 22 N.C. App. 663 (1974).

265. S.L. 1995-429.

266. 191 N.C. App. 776 (2008).

267. State v. Crowder, 208 N.C. App. 723 (2010).

268. State v. Boone, 225 N.C. App. 423 (2013) (emphasis in original) ("Absent *any* evidence of a required payment schedule . . . conclusory testimony that defendant was in arrears is insufficient to support a finding that defendant had willfully violated the terms of his probation by failing to pay the required fees or perform community service on time.").

269. State v. Krider, ___ N.C. App. ___, 810 S.E.2d 828, *aff'd*, ___ N.C. ___, ___ S.E.2d ___ (Sept. 21, 2018).

IX. Appeals

When a district court judge activates a probationer's suspended sentence or imposes special probation, the defendant may appeal to the superior court for a de novo revocation hearing. There is no statutory right to appeal other modifications of probation,[270] including CRV.[271]

For violating behavior that occurred on or after December 1, 2013, there is no right to appeal to superior court for a defendant who waives his or her right to a violation hearing in district court.[272] It is not clear, however, what constitutes waiver of a violation hearing. For instance, mere admission to a violation arguably is not a waiver if the probationer asks to be heard on the sanction that will be imposed in response to the violation. A district court probationer wanting to preserve his or her right to appeal to superior court should take that ambiguity into account when admitting to a violation, perhaps qualifying any admission with an express statement that the district court hearing has not been waived.

If, at a de novo hearing, the superior court continues the defendant on probation under the same or modified conditions, the case is considered to be a superior court case from that point forward; all future proceedings in the case are handled in superior court.[273]

When a violation hearing for a Class H or I felony pled in district court is held in district court, the appeal of any revocation order or modification imposing special probation is de novo to superior court, not to the court of appeals.[274] By contrast, if the district court exercises jurisdiction to revoke probation in a case supervised under G.S. 7A-272(e), which governs supervision of certain drug treatment court or therapeutic court cases, appeal of an order revoking probation is to the appellate division.[275]

When a superior court judge revokes probation or imposes special probation, the defendant may appeal to the appellate division under G.S. 15A-1347 and G.S. 7A-27. There is no statutory right to appeal other modifications of probation, including CRV.

No statute explicitly governs the timing of probation appeals or the court's authority to impose conditions of release during their pendency. In the absence of statutes specific to probation violations, the provisions governing appeals of convictions probably apply. Notice of appeal from district court to superior court probably must come

---

270. State v. Edgerson, 164 N.C. App. 712 (2004).

271. State v. Romero, 228 N.C. App. 348, 366, n.1 (2013). *Romero* involved a non-terminal CRV (that is, a CRV period that did not use up the defendant's entire suspended sentence). The *Romero* court included a footnote noting that the court expressly declined to offer any opinion on whether a defendant would have a right to appeal a terminal CRV, which is functionally similar to revocation from the defendant's point of view.

272. G.S. 15A-1347; S.L. 2013-385.

273. G.S. 15A-1347.

274. State v. Hooper, 358 N.C. 122 (2004).

275. G.S. 7A-271(f).

orally or in writing to the clerk within 10 days of entry of judgment.[276] For appeals from superior court to the appellate division, it appears that Rule 4(a) of the Rules of Appellate Procedure requires oral notice of appeal upon revocation or the filing of a notice of appeal within 14 days after entry of the judgment revoking probation.[277]

Appeal of a district court violation hearing stays any activated sentence or split sentence, but the judge may order appropriate conditions of release pending the de novo hearing in superior court.[278] Appeal of a superior court violation hearing to the appellate division stays the imposition of any split sentence, but stays confinement on an activated sentence only if the judge allows release during the pendency of the appeal, typically (if at all) through an appeal bond.[279] If the court does allow release pending appeal, probation supervision continues under the same conditions until the probation period expires or the appeal is disposed of, whichever comes first.[280]

If a defendant appeals an activation of a sentence as a result of a finding of a violation of probation by the district or superior court and is released pursuant to Article 26 of G.S. Chapter 15A, probation supervision will continue under the same conditions until the expiration of the period of probation or disposition of the appeal, whichever comes first.

When appealing an order activating a suspended sentence, the defendant generally may not challenge the original judgment suspending sentence, as doing so is an impermissible collateral attack.[281] That prohibition extends to jurisdictional challenges to the underlying conviction made for the first time upon appeal of a revocation, such as arguments that the original charging instrument was defective.[282] (This rule against raising jurisdictional arguments for the first time on appeal does not, however, bar consideration of those issues at the revocation hearing itself in the trial division.) A limited exception to the rule against collateral attacks is that the defendant may, upon appeal of a probation revocation, argue for the first time that he or she was unconstitutionally denied counsel at the original trial.[283]

---

276. G.S. 15A-1431(c).

277. *See* State v. Long, 220 N.C. App. 139 (2012) (granting a defendant's petition for writ of certiorari when defendant counsel failed to file written notice of appeal of a judgment revoking probation within the time set out in Rule 4(a)).

278. G.S. 15A-1431(f1).

279. G.S. 15A-1451(a).

280. G.S. 15A-1347(c).

281. State v. Holmes, 361 N.C. 410 (2007); State v. Noles, 12 N.C. App. 676 (1971).

282. State v. Pennell, 367 N.C. 466 (2014).

283. State v. Neeley, 307 N.C. 247 (1982).